Practical Biblical Prayer

MARK AND ALISON RUTLAND

Radiant Life

1445 North Boonville Avenue
Springfield, MO 65802-1894

02-0133

STAFF

National Director: Arlyn R. Pember
Editor in Chief: John T. Maempa
Adult Projects Editor Paul W. Smith
Product Coordinator: Robert L. Walden
Cover Design: Craig W. Schutt
Inside Design: Randy M. Clute

Photo Credits:
©1999 Comstock, Inc: Cover, Cleo Photography: Cover, 4,
©1994 PhotoDisc Inc.: 14, ©1998 PhotoDisc Inc.: 37, 44, 50, 64, 79, 86,
©Digital Vision: 72, © 1996 Diamar Portfolios 21, 29,
AG World Missions, 57

People pictured in the photographs in this book are models depicting roles. They are not
the people referred to in the text.

"Scripture taken from the HOLY BIBLE, NEW INTERNATIONAL VERSION.
Copyright © 1973, 1978, 1984 International Bible Society. Used by permission
of Zondervan Bible Publishers."

©2002 by the Gospel Publishing House
Springfield, Missouri 65802-1894

ISBN 0-88243-133-1
Printed in the United States of America

A Leader's Guide for individual or group study with this book is available
(order number 02-0233) 088243-233-8

CONTENTS

WELCOME TO THE

SPIRITUAL DISCOVERY SERIES

We are glad you have chosen to study with us. We believe the discoveries you make through the use of the *Spiritual Discovery Series* will positively impact your life.

The *Spiritual Discovery Series* will challenge the user to ask questions of the biblical text, discover principles from the text, and make personal application of those truths. The Bible is the text. This guide is a tool for study.

The *Spiritual Discovery Series* is designed for use in either individual or group settings. Individuals will be excited by the discoveries made possible through a structured inductive study. Sunday School classes and other groups will find the *Spiritual Discovery Series* a valuable tool for promoting enlightened discussions centered on biblical truth.

How To Use This Study Guide

1 **Pray before beginning each study session.** Ask the Holy Spirit to illuminate your mind.

---

2 **Choose a translation of the Bible which you trust and can understand.** It will be helpful to have more than one translation available to aid your understanding of the biblical text.

---

3 **The Bible is your primary text.** Avoid using commentaries or reference books until after completing your own study. Reference works are best used to confirm your findings. On occasion, the study guide will direct you to use reference material. This is done when special insights are necessary for proper interpretation.

---

4 **Read the assigned biblical text at least twice before answering any questions.** This will provide an overview and focus on God's Word.

---

5 **Concentrate on the biblical passage which you are studying.** It is tempting to jump from one passage of Scripture to another in an attempt to make spiritual connections.

---

6 **Seek tangible ways to apply the principles gleaned from each study.** Bible study should never result in "head knowledge" alone. Bible study should lead to action.

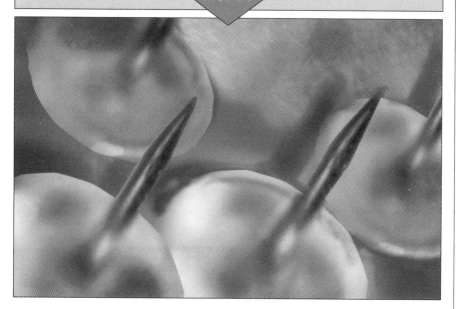

THE PRACTICE OF PRAYER: GETTING DOWN TO BRASS TACKS

E ver body talkin' 'bout heaven ain't goin' there" (*American Negro Songs*, John W. Work). These words of a 19th century American Negro spiritual are convicting and practical. A major university in the United States offers a course titled "Theory of Soccer." What a ludicrous idea! Surely at some point, someone ought to stop theorizing about the cultural implications of the sport and actually kick the ball. Many in the church have confused talking with doing. Nowhere is this confusion more tragic than when it comes to prayer. Talking about prayer is not the same as praying.

In any field, from architecture to basket weaving, theory will only go so far, and then the doing must begin. When the disciples asked Jesus to teach them to pray, his response was apparently devoid of theory, offering instead, a model, imminently practical. Jesus did not teach about prayer; He just showed them how to do it.

This entire study is an attempt to get believers to "do" prayer. Maybe we have allowed this entire arena of the Christian life to become a mere theory zone. Why do we talk about prayer so much and do it so little?

THE PRACTICE OF PRAYER

Breaking Through the Spiritual Language Barrier

A missionary work team was set to begin laying block for a new church when the team leader, a pastor, called for prayer. One of the workers stated an unfortunate, yet commonly held attitude toward prayer. "You do the praying, Preacher, we'll lay the block."

Some people do not feel they can access prayer because they are not "spiritual." Sometimes the language around prayer implies that it is "just for preachers." We must shatter the mystique and get down to brass tacks.

✎ 1. Read Luke 11:1-4. In which ways does Jesus' language seem "spiritual" and in which way is it practical?

_____

_____

_____

Some believers feel unable to enter the work of prayer because they are not "great" Christians. Even the phrase, "The Lord's Prayer" may make it seem that only He can pray it worthily. Some have called Luke 11:1-4, the "Apostles' Prayer." A better name is the "Believers' Prayer."

✎ 2. Read James 5:17. How does James' description of the great prophet Elijah make him more human? How does that encourage "regular" Christians to pray?

_____

_____

_____

At the essence of all pagan worship is the belief that by making worship more complicated the gods or spirits will be pleased. This conviction is at the root of paganism's emphasis on formulas, rules, laws, secret ceremonies, and complicated worship practices known only to the priestly cult. Even in non-Christian religions like Islam, one can observe an emphasis on times, ways, and rituals of prayer. In Matthew 6:7, Jesus debunks this theory and calls instead for simple, direct prayer.

✎ 3 . Read Matthew 6:7-8. Pagans have no concept of a "Father God," but believe in contrary spirits that must be pacified. How does Jesus' understanding of the fatherhood of God affect the way we pray?

_____

_____

_____

There will always be those who think themselves more or less spiritual than others based on outward superficialities. More modest hearts are easily impressed with the religiosity of others, and the sanctimonious with their own. In Matthew 6:1-6, Jesus called simple folk to pray with humble simplicity.

PRACTICAL PERSONAL BENEFITS OF REGULAR PRAYER

✎ 4. Read Matthew 6:1-6. Why does Jesus connect false piety and empty prayer? Is there ever a place for public prayer? Was Jesus forbidding it or teaching it?

_____

_____

_____

"What's in it for me?" has become the unwholesome anthem of modern civilization that has misplaced its own nobility and the joy of sacrificial servanthood. It is the unfortunate yet predictable fruit of western culture's exaltation of selfishness. On the other hand, if we are honest with ourselves, there is a need in all of us to understand the practical fruit, expected from any endeavor. Maybe another, better way of asking the question is, "What good will this do me?"

✎ 5. Read Proverbs 31, taking special note of verses 28-31, the catalogue of the rewards for the diligent. Is the concept of reward and punishment elsewhere in the Bible? Do the rewards of Proverbs 31:28-31 also apply to diligence in prayer? Why?

_____

_____

_____

One Christian businessman in Africa said, "I can more easily convert a diligent pagan employee than I can teach diligence to a slothful Christian employee." Discipline is its own reward. It tends toward order, structure, success, fulfillment, and even prosperity. A regular, disciplined prayer life brings with it the benefit of simply adding to the "discipline mechanism" of our character. People disciplined in one area tend to be disciplined in others.

✎ 6. Read Proverbs 24:3-34. Rewrite verses 30-34 as they might read if verse 30 began, "I went by the field of the disciplined...." Do these practical benefits translate in a disciplined prayer life? Use another piece of paper if needed.

_____

_____

_____

_____

Beyond discipline for its own sake, regular prayer works a work in us as believers. There are needed changes in us that can be accomplished by the Spirit much more easily if we are in regular prayer. Forget for a moment the issue of how prayer changes circumstances. That is next. For now, think of the practical personal benefits that arise out of the reality that prayer changes us. One Mexican pastor testified, "I prayed for years that God would change my mother-in-law, but He did not. In the process, however, I found grace to love her as she is."

7. Read 1 Kings 19:4-21. After Elijah's encounter with God at Horeb, what in the circumstance was changed? Was Ahab changed? Jezebel? The nation? What about Elijah?

_____

_____

_____

_____

Elijah was so depressed by the situation in his country and the threats against his life that he prayed to die. The tendency to depression is not, in itself, a sin. But it can either separate us from God or cause us to pray with greater passion.

8. How did Elijah realize the practical personal benefits of prayer?

A. Spiritually: _____

_____

B. Emotionally: _____

_____

C. Relationally: (read verses 15-21 again) _____

_____

PRACTICAL KINGDOM BENEFITS

The story is told about a World War II battalion commander who was ordered to attack a certain town in France. An airplane overhead radioed specific directions to the colonel's headquarters. These he consistently ignored and finally, after several hours of pitched battle, retreated. When the pilot landed, he demanded to know why they had retreated with victory at hand. The colonel said, "It didn't look like we were winning where I was standing."

"Yes," said the pilot, "but from the sky I could see that the enemy was getting ready to retreat, and I can see things from up there that you can't see down here!"

Prayer works. That is the bottom line. If prayer accomplished nothing in us (which we have seen it does), it still has practical kingdom benefits. Sometimes we just retreat too soon!

✎ **9. Can you name some specific historical and/or biblical events changed by prayer?**

_____

_____

_____

_____

We live in the time of drink machines and "fast food." Our western mindset is one of instant gratification. For that reason, it is often easier to generate ongoing prayer campaigns in the Third World. People more accustomed to waiting are less temperamental about waiting on God.

✎ **10. How has the idea of "claiming things by faith" eroded our ability to "pray through?" Read Luke 18:1-8. Is Jesus' teaching on the character of God or perseverance in prayer?**

_____

_____

_____

_____

_____

A way to strengthen our faith in the practical results of prayer is by "keeping score." We need to rehearse the results of the past in order to be encouraged for future prayers.

✎ **11. On another sheet of paper or a posterboard, design your personal "scorecard," where you will list prayers and their results. Share some past victories with others who may need encouragement. List some prayer requests here just to get started.**

_____

_____

_____

_____

Professional basketball player, Karl Malone, once said, "The better I get, the better I get." That is also true in prayer. Once you start getting answers, you get them faster and more fully.

✎ 12. Why do you think Christ had such instant power in healing? Is there a connotation between how much He prayed in private and how fruitfully He prayed in public?

_____

_____

_____

_____

There is great practical kingdom benefit in answered prayer beyond simply getting the answers we need. Every time God answers prayer, He gets glorified in both the spiritual and temporal domains.

✎ 13. Read Acts 5:12-14. How do unbelievers react when they see the power of God? They do not always get saved. Are there other ways they glorify God? How should believers glorify God when He answers prayer?

_____

_____

_____

_____

A teenager, David, called on his friend John to go play soccer, but John declined, saying he needed to work with his father instead. "Is he making you?" David asked. "No," John said. "But I know he wants me to."

✎ 14. Read Acts 9:10-15. Why does God respond to Saul's prayer? What insight does the passage give to Ananias' prayer life?

_____

_____

_____

_____

SUMMARY

Prayer is not just for the spiritual "super heroes." Normal believers who will just pray regularly, at the level they can today, will find benefits in their own lives, get answers from God, and glorify His name. We must be practical. Being "down to earth" in prayer is exactly the way to reach "up to heaven."

LET'S REVIEW

1. Why do we need to break the overly spiritualized veil over prayer?

_____

_____

_____

2. What are some practical benefits in "keeping on" in prayer?

_____

_____

_____

3. What are the top two priorities in hoped-for change when we pray?

_____

_____

_____

_____

4. What is God's priority in calling us to prayer?

_____

_____

_____

_____

5. "Keeping score" seems a little crass. Why keep track of answered prayer?

_____

_____

_____

PhotoDisc

BEHIND THE VEIL: UNDERSTANDING WHY PRAYER WORKS

A farmer in Peru was given a new generator by a foreign visitor. The visitor demonstrated the proper mixture of gasoline and oil on which the machine ran, but the proud owner decided to save on oil and fed it only gasoline. On a return trip, the visitor found the generator burned and useless.

The generator was repaired. This time the foreigner explained not only the required mixture, but also *why* the oil additive was necessary. The oil, that previously made no sense to the Peruvian farmer, was never left out again. A basic understanding of how the machine worked increased the likelihood of its being well cared for.

This principle is true in most disciplines of life, including prayer. Many believers are hindered in their devotional access to God because of bad concepts of who He is and why He listens to prayer.

GETTING A RIGHT PICTURE OF GOD

How one approaches God in prayer is a product, to a degree, of how we understand who He is. A young girl who has been mistreated by her father is likely to be hampered in an atmosphere of rigid legalism and may never be able to truly rest in God's presence. How we pray may be more a factor of our functional theology— how we relate to God— than what we say we believe. Often Christians seek to fulfill a checklist of spiritual activities to be OK in the eyes of the church community. This mind-set leads to much activity without real prayer—communication with God. We must recognize our "prayer times" are mislabeled unless we touch God.

✎1. **Read Matthew 6:5. What misguided view of God would make people pray incorrectly? What mistaken concepts of God have you encountered?**

_____

_____

✎2. **Listed below are some specific misconceptions of God. How does each one affect the way people pray or don't pray?**

A. God as the "Force" _____

_____

B. Legalism _____

_____

C. Humanism _____

_____

D. An angry God _____

_____

E. A bellhop God _____

_____

F. A disinterested God _____

_____

G. An old, senile God _____

_____

H. A powerless God _____

_____

Humans are seeking to find a sense of unity of self. Modern western culture has fragmented the family and community, making this search even more difficult. For believers, an understanding of the wholeness and integrity of God's person is the starting point to finding personal wholeness.

An absurdly misspelled sign on a small church read, "Holey Ghost Revival Now in Progress." This would be funny if it were not sad. "Holey" actually means "full of holes," the exact opposite of "holy," that not only means "exalted," but also means "perfect, entire, pure." There is nothing wanting in God that could be added to make Him "more God."

Likewise, there is nothing superfluous that could be removed to make Him more pure. He is wholly God—an altogether perfect, pure, and holy God.

3. **Read Exodus 3:13,14. Notice that Moses asked God for a fresh revelation of His divine nature. Was this for the Egyptians or for the people of God? Who most needs a fresh revelation of God today—the church or the world? Why?**

_____

_____

_____

God calls himself "I AM THAT I AM" (Exodus 3:14, KJV). God cannot ever be other than himself. He is whole, holy, and wholly bound by that character. One of the other great truths about God is that He is omnipresent. Combining those two truths we see that God can never be fractionalized. He is never partial, never one way here and another way there, and never ever do we encounter only part of God. He is not only everywhere; He is wholly everywhere and everywhere holy.

4. **Why was this particular revelation so important to Moses and Israel at that time in their history?**

_____

_____

_____

Many people are reluctant to bother God in prayer with the small details of their lives. They feel others may need His attention for greater matters. But, if God is I AM to every believer, then all of God's attention, thought, energy, and love are wholly present with every one of us all the time. Some see God as a frazzled telephone operator sitting at the cosmic switchboard terrified that all the lights will go on at once. God has only one line—He is at one end and you are at the other.

5. **What are some other views of prayer that may hinder believers?**

_____

_____

_____

_____

NOW THAT YOU HAVE GOD'S FULL ATTENTION: WHY SHOULD HE LISTEN?

For God to be holy means that He is always the same. That He is wholly omnipresent means that He is always the same and entirely present—everywhere at the same time. This means that everyone who prays to God has His full attention! If that is true (and it is), why should He listen to sinful humanity?

✎ 6. Read 1 John 4:7-14. What is the essential quality of God's character?

_____

_____

Therefore, we can say God listens because He _____humanity all the time in a personal way. He loves fully, constantly and eternally. List yourself and your loved ones.

_____

_____

_____

God also listens when we pray for the same reason He created mankind to begin with. He enjoys the fellowship. God wants us to pray obediently and relationally. God listens because He likes to hear us talk.

✎ 7. In last week's lesson you read Acts 9:10,11. Read it again in the King James Version, noting the word "behold." Why is the word "behold" used?

_____

_____

God the Father listens because of who He is. He also listens because of who God the Son is. Read Hebrews 4:16; 5:6; and 7:25. Now fill in the blanks in the following sentence.

✎ 8. God _____ when we pray _____ about our

_____, because His _____, our _____

_____, is _____ for us at the same time.

Now we can begin to add the elements together to get a more complete picture. When we pray, a holy and loving God listens because He wants a relationship with us and because His Son acts as our Priest for us. But there is one very important element missing! For our High Priest, the Lord Jesus Christ, to make our prayers heard to the eternal God, there had to have been an eternal sacrifice—the sacrifice of His blood!

✎ 9. Read Hebrews 9:14. How does Christ's sacrifice affect our relationship with God?

_____

_____

_____

GOD HEARS, BUT DOES HE RESPOND?

A man was watching a football game on television when his wife asked him to carry a box too heavy for her. She repeated the request four times before she finally cried out, "Didn't you hear me?"

"Yes," he said. "I heard you. I'm just not responding."

Sometimes we get the idea that God is like a preoccupied husband unwilling to rouse himself and act. We now know why God hears us, but do we have any hope that He is moved by prayer? Deism says that God has set in motion all the laws by which the universe now runs and He refuses to interact with human history. Contrast that with John Wesley's contention, "There are some things God will not do until we pray."

✎ 10. Read Zechariah 10:1-6. From verse 6, list at least four things God said He would do for Israel in answer to prayer and why. How can each of these be applied to believers today?

A. I will_____

_____

B. I will_____

_____

C. I will_____

_____

D. I will _____

_____

because, I am the _____ their God, and will _____ them.

If God hears us and acts in response to our prayer of faith, can we count on Him to always do what we want, when we want it, in the way we imagine? Balance is crucial, but it must be true balance. If we think faith is the ultimate power in the universe, we will become presumptuous in prayer; but if we pray without faith, we will see few results. The true balance to faith is the sovereignty of God.

✎ 11. Read Luke 4:9-13. What is the real temptation that was set before Christ? How did He answer it?

_____

_____

_____

_____

How we pray is a result of our functional theology and does not necessarily come from our stated doctrine. One who never prays does not really believe it works. One who whines and begs and blames God does not truly pray to a holy God of love. One who "claims everything by faith" and never patiently waits on God does not have a balanced understanding of God's sovereign will.

✎ 12. List three reasons why God hears prayer, and three non-negotiable parts of your functional theology of prayer.

_____

_____

_____

_____

_____

_____

SUMMARY

A correct understanding of prayer is essential to building an effective prayer life. Not mere theory, but preeminently practical, good theology is the basis of effective prayer. We must pray to the right God and pray to God right. When we do, we know that He listens and acts in answer to such prayer. "Prayer works" is not church rhetoric. It is the practical hope of believers praying practical prayers to a responsive yet sovereign God.

LET'S REVIEW

1. Give some synonyms for holy. Why does the concept affect prayer?

_____

_____

_____

_____

2. Why do we need a high priest?

_____

_____

_____

3. Why is the blood of Jesus important to prayer?

_____

_____

_____

_____

4. God hears, but does He respond? Give Scripture references to show what the Bible says about this.

_____

_____

_____

_____

5. How might a wrong concept of God hinder prayer?

_____

_____

_____

_____

STUDY 3

PRAYER ADMINISTRATION

A certain medium-sized corporation stated in its annual report, "We are in excellent condition, continuing to do what we have always done—turn a profit and make a good product. No major changes are anticipated."

Eighteen months later the company was bankrupt, the CEO forced to retire and four top executives fired. Why? They violated all four fundamentals of good administration: analysis, goal setting, planning, and evaluation.

Unwilling to face the truth about its financial condition, executives dismissed the need for new goals (analysis) to lead the corporation into necessary change. Without goals there could be no formulated plan (goal setting) to "get there." How could there be strategy (planning) if there is no destination? Finally, complacency ate away the company's goals and objectivity (evaluation), which were despised as negative and unnecessary.

Many believers hurt themselves in prayer with bad administration they would never allow in business. With these four fundamentals of good administration, Christians can find progress in most stagnant areas of their spiritual formation—especially prayer. Some believers, thinking they are spiritually healthy, actually find themselves on the verge of "prayer bankruptcy."

ADMINISTRATION AND SPIRITUALITY

There is much to be said for spontaneity, and liberty is one hallmark of passionate, Pentecostal praying. But organization doesn't have to inhibit spirituality. In fact, structure in prayer can do much to preserve the lasting effects of a spiritual advance.

John Wesley and George Whitefield were contemporaries in 18th century England. Whitefield was by far the more famous and talented. The anointing upon his booming and enviable voice made him the most popular preacher in the world. But at the end of his life, Whitefield realized while Wesley's organizational skills had preserved that revival, he mournfully called his own ministry "a rope of sand." Becoming practical in prayer administration does not mean working against joyful liberty. In fact, practicality may empower liberty and consolidate spiritual gains.

1. Read Proverbs 30:25-28. What corporate skills are personified by each of these four creatures? Why are such practical skills taught in a spiritual book like the Bible?

_____

_____

_____

Prayer Analysis

The four elements of successful administration are analysis, goal setting, planning, and evaluation. The first of these (analysis), will be useless without a realistic idea of how much time you can spend in prayer, and that reality must be without guilt. There is no "right" or "biblical" goal in prayer except to pray without ceasing. An hour a day or 5 hours a day are man's rules, not God's. God wants you to be realistic about how much time you spend in prayer. If you currently pray a minute a day, and as a result of this study you start praying 5 minutes a day, you have made five times as much progress as before. Reality—the amount of time you *actually* spend in prayer—is the power of analysis—how much time you *could* spend in prayer.

2. Read Proverbs 27:23. How does "knowing the state of thy flocks," relate to analysis and reality? How can this proverb be applied to prayer?

_____

_____

_____

_____

Below are five questions to help you to do an analysis of your prayers. Remember that self-condemnation and inflated answers are counterproductive. Be honest! (Suggestion: be conservative as well.)

3. Prayer Self-Analysis: How much are you praying now?

_____ minutes per ○ day ○ week ○ month

Using a scale of 1 to 10 (with 1 being ineffective and 10 being very effective), how effective are your prayers; that is, how well do you feel your prayers touch the heart of God?

_____ Your score

What do you pray about the most? List three areas.

1. _____ 2. _____ 3. _____

When and where do you pray the most?

_____

What "form" of prayer do you use most?

○ Praise ○ Petition ○ Tongues ○ Rambling ○ A List

SETTING PRAYER GOALS

One soccer coach in Nigeria said, "If your goal is to get better you will probably get worse. If your goal is to score twice as frequently as last year, you will probably get better." What the coach seems to be saying is that vague, unmeasurable goals tend to be ignored. Specific, practical, achievable goals motivate us to a plan of action that will lead to "real" results.

4. Following the sound advice of that Nigerian coach, list general kinds of measurable prayer goals—not specific goals, but areas of measurable improvement. For example, a construction firm might have goals such as 1) faster completion of projects; 2) better estimations of cost and materials; 3) a wider profit margin; 4) more units built. Now list some for your own prayer life:

A. _____

_____

B. _____

_____

C. _____

_____

D. _____

_____

5. Review your list in item 4. Name potential hindrances to each area of possible advancement. For example, in the construction firm model: 1) faster completion might be slowed by too few workers, but 3) a wider profit margin might then be reduced by more workers.

Possible Areas of Advancement	Potential Hindrances
A. _____	A. _____
B. _____	B. _____
C. _____	C. _____
D. _____	D. _____

6. For each area listed above set at least one practical, attainable goal. Keep the balance between setting impossible goals and setting goals that do not stretch you at all. Goal setting in any discipline is much art as science. If the goals are too high you may become discouraged and drop out. But, if the goals are too easy, complacency may set in and lead to disinterest or even self-satisfaction, which are progress killers.

Areas of Advancement	Goals
A. _____	1. _____
	2. _____
	3. _____
B. _____	1. _____
	2. _____
	3. _____
C. _____	1. _____
	2. _____
	3. _____
D. _____	1. _____
	2. _____
	3. _____

Boiler Plate Language

Look back over the list of goals and check for wording that is vague and over-spiritualized. (Example) "I will do spiritual warfare in the heavenlies until Satan trembles." That's fine, but how would you know if Satan trembles, and how would you measure your progress?

✎7. State your goal for prayer in the coming year. State this goal realistically in terms of time, frequency, expected outcome, and method.

A poor example: I will pray more, longer, better and get more answers.

A good example: I will expand my daily prayer time to 10 minutes every other day, and I want to see three specific prayers answered before the year is over by telling God in specific terms what my requests are.

PRAYER GOAL

(Fill in the blanks)
This coming year my top three goals in prayer are to pray _____ minutes
(time)

_____(daily, weekly), and my goal is to see divine response to
(frequency)

_____specific prayers by
(outcome)

_____.
(method)

BUILDING YOUR PRAYER PLAN

One American business professor said the two major causes of failure in business are strategies that do not connect to stated goals, and lack of creativity. In World War I, English generals unnecessarily sacrificed their soldiers at the battle of Gallipoli Peninsula because of these two failures. The battle itself was not essential to the overall victory of the war, and the plan lacked creative response to the modern technology of the day. Marching across open terrain on the peninsula, soldiers were slaughtered because they faced machine guns, not cavalry as in previous wars. In the same manner, prayers that lack goals and creativity may also be doomed to fail.

Having established prayer goals for the coming year, here are some ideas to help you develop a strategy that will further those goals and respond creatively to your current lifestyle and surroundings.

Be Creative

Remember there is more than one time of day and method of praying. Prayer cards or lists help many. Some pray at different times. One man in Africa wrote that on Monday, Wednesday, and Friday he prayed as he walked to the bus stop. On Tuesdays and Thursdays he had an extra hour in his house, and would pray as he watered his garden. One man in India prays every day as he dresses, each item of clothing reminding him of some particular need. An American housewife waits until her family is gone and prays at mid-morning. A busy college girl in Florida prays 1 minute before each class, 1 minute before meals and 5 minutes at bedtime—an estimated 15 minutes a day—then adds a half hour on Saturday.

8. When will you pray? _____

How long will you pray? _____

How much of an increase from what you are currently praying is that?

_____

Are there some other creative ways you can pray? _____

_____

_____

_____

_____

Enlist Help

A great distance runner from Kenya said just having someone to run alongside made him a more determined runner. "They cannot move my legs for me. I must do that. But the comfort of their presence makes me refuse to quit." You need people to pray for your prayer life, to call occasionally and check on your progress, and even pray with you from time to time.

9. Read James 5:16. List several people who might be willing to pray for your prayer life.

_____

_____

_____

_____

_____

Now call them and any others you think of. Will any of them "check on you" and will any meet you occasionally for encouraging prayer?

Document the Process

Use your personal prayer calendar that you will receive in class to record your progress. Do not be intimidated! Mark on the calendar which days you will pray and how long. If there are special notations such as creative reminders or particular times of day or places, be prepared to note those as well. Each day plan to record your actual accomplishment. Do not pad the record! No one will see this but you.

✎10. Read Hebrews 12:1. Is prayer a part of the race described here? How shall we run it?

_____

_____

_____

_____

Get Started

The time-honored cadence for runners to start a race is:
Runners, take your marks....Get set....Go!
On "Runners, take your marks," the athletes get ready, move to the starting blocks, fasten their minds on the race, and take a last second to calm themselves. At "get set" they actually get in the blocks, poise themselves for the start, and gather every muscle for the gun. If all that is not done in order and on command, the starting pistol may find them unprepared. It is an ancient ritual of track and field from which we can learn much.

Many people plunge into some new spiritual discipline unprepared and find frustration and defeat. Get in the rhythm of the race mentally before the gun goes off.

✎11. Runners, take your marks: Think about these plans again. Check your goals. Can you do it? Of course you can! Pray about your goals and make sure your support team is in place.

Get Set: Set the date (not today, but at your next class meeting) for the beginning of this new spiritual race. I will begin on_____

Go! Start next time your class meets!

SUMMARY

One corporate CEO in New York said that honest evaluation is essential to ongoing success. Without it, he said, we may be failing without knowing or succeeding and never celebrating.

Using your "Prayer Planner," do three levels of evaluation: monthly, quarterly, and a final one at the end of a year. Remember, do not let condemnation over unachieved goals cause you to drop out of the race. Instead, let honest evaluation instruct you in where and how to improve. If your "support team" is trusted and intimate enough, share the results with them and get their advice and prayer. Your class leader will guide you in this.

LET'S REVIEW

1. What are the four elements of successful prayer administration?

_____

_____

_____

_____

2. Why is prayer organization so important?

_____

_____

_____

3. Note some prayer phrases you feel have vague wording. Now rewrite them, using creative language.

_____

_____

_____

4. What are some different times/ways to pray, or methods of prayer you can think of, besides church services or meals?

_____

_____

_____

5. Think of some people in your life who exemplify the qualities of good prayer administration. List some of those qualities you'd like to incorporate into your own prayer life.

_____

_____

_____

DIAMAR Portfolios

THE POSSIBILITIES OF DAILY PRAYER PATTERNS

An elderly woman sits on the third floor balcony of a shabby apartment house in a poor area of Rome. She vacantly watches several youths kick a soccer ball in the squalid street below as she fingers her rosary beads. From any distance at all, an observer could never see the slight movement of her lips.

In Jerusalem, an Arab driver for the Mahfonz Tour Bus Company watches patiently as his cargo of elderly, overweight American Christians disembark to trudge up the Mount of Olives. After a while they will reboard, their arms and handbags bulging with olive wood camels. As he watches them go, the prayer call blares from loudspeakers atop the nearby minaret, and he dismounts to join several other drivers, who pitch aside their cigarettes and spread their prayer rugs. He will go through the entire Islamic ritual of prayer: kneeling, standing, and kneeling again in exact synchronization with the other drivers. He has plenty of time. It takes these Christians a long time to buy camels.

PRAYER OR RITUAL?

There is in prayer, as in all things religious, a delicate balance to be maintained between the undisciplined life of prayerlessness and the "structure" of form without power. Mere repetition, dogged obedience to an "entirely other" set of rules, can hardly be of much value in terms of exploring many of prayer's higher and inner blessings.

By the same token, many western Protestants, so contemptuous of slavish religiosity, have little regular prayer life at all. Lacking discipline, they hope liberty will motivate where structure and form do not dictate. Instead, they find only scattered and undisciplined prayer lives filled with an uncertain spiritual vocabulary and hardly any of the accumulated weight of repeated petition. In other words, they pray tentative, wandering prayers of occasional passion but little of the concentrated, ongoing intensity that a pattern can provide.

1. Read Matthew 6:7-13. Jesus denounced "heathen" or "pagan" prayer for its confidence in what? _____ He then proceeded to give us a prayer model or a suggested pattern of His own. Could "The Lord's Prayer" ever become a "pagan" prayer?_____

How? _____

_____

_____

_____

Why, then, did Jesus give us a pattern at all? _____

_____

_____

_____

There are advantages, in any area of life, to doing the same thing pretty much the same way, most of the time. Otherwise, why do athletes practice skills repeatedly, paratroopers leap from tall towers dozens of times before ever getting in a plane, and elementary school children write thousands of "A's" and "B's?"

2. List several advantages to a "pattern" in learning and practice. In other words, what do many repetitions of certain motions accomplish in, say, golf or cooking?

_____

_____

_____

_____

3. In what ways do such repetitions inhibit or liberate creativity? A basketball player may shoot a thousand baskets from the same spot in practice, but in a game that same shot may look completely different. Which player is more likely to meet the challenge creatively—the one who has shot a thousand baskets the same way, or the one who has mastered many different kinds of shots?

_____

_____

_____

THREE BIBLICAL PATTERNS IN PRAYER

The "Lord's Prayer," so called, might more appropriately be called the "Disciples' Prayer" since the Lord gave it to us, His disciples. Be that as it may, the "Lord's Prayer" and other prayer patterns used appropriately can form the pegs upon which we hang our most impassioned prayers. The point must be clear, however, that merely repeating these words will prove less effective than using the structure of the pattern and "fleshing it out" as the Holy Spirit gives us liberty.

We want to identify the structural elements or divisions of this pattern, pray the specific words once, or twice. Then, inside each division, pray to God as He leads us in prayer. Read Matthew 6:9-13 and outline the prayer pattern.

Praise

Matthew 6:9—Praise for

A. The fatherhood of God
B. God's heavenly or spiritual quality and abode
C. God's hallowed (holy) name.

4. What is the central theme of these three praises? These are praises to God for His

_____

_____

_____

As you pray this first verse, you have an initial platform on which to construct your own praise for God's character and goodness. Let your spirit go. Use biblical and nonbiblical language of praise for God. Concentrate on "who" God is. Three elements are obvious; list three praiseworthy adjectives for each of them.

5. God's fatherhood is...

_____

_____

God's heavenly nature is ...

_____

_____

_____

God's holy name is ...

_____

_____

_____

Petition

Read Matthew 6:10-13. This is the section of the prayer in which our petitions are not only appropriate but also expected. Note that this section is the longest because Jesus knew that our needs are greater than our capacity for pure praise. How practical Jesus was!

6. **Depending on how you read verses 10-13, there are four to six separate petitions. How many can you identify?**

1. _____

2. _____

3. _____

4. _____

5. _____

6. _____

As we pray these specific petitions we should "flesh them out" by making application to immediate needs in our own lives. "Thy kingdom come. Thy will be done..." in the life of any unsaved neighbor, should be followed by prayers for that neighbor's welfare as the Spirit leads.

"Give us this day our daily bread" is an obvious moment to pray about financial and/or employment issues. First, pray the words Jesus gave, and then let the words guide you into a wider expression of the implications of those words.

7. **Read the first part of Matthew 6:13. Think of circumstances in which this prayer concerning temptation and deliverance might be especially important.**

_____

_____

_____

Have you ever found such an occasion in your own life?

_____

_____

Submission

Read the second half of Matthew 6:13. Now read 1 Chronicles 29:11 and note the similarities. Jesus was evidently using a "prayer pattern" himself in teaching us one. The point here is submission to the kingship of God. I have praised You and I have given You my petitions but the bottom line is—You are the King, not me.

✎ 8. Why does it help to add the words power and glory at this point?

_____

_____

Why remember God's power at the end of a prayer filled with petitions?

_____

_____

Why mention glory at the end? Is there any way you can see that as a particularly humble prayer?

_____

_____

THE PRAYER OF SPIRITUAL ARMOR

Read Ephesians 6:13-17. Many Christians have found it encouraging and strengthening to begin the day by "putting on the armor of God." To pray through this famous passage from Ephesians phrase-by-phrase lends structure to a prayer of faith for many elements of the spiritual life from protection to holiness. There are seven (7) pieces of armor listed here, six defensive and one offensive, through which we can find a useful daily pattern of daily prayer. There are two great advantages to using the Christian armor prayer pattern.

A Visual Aid to Faith

We are, in general, visual not conceptual thinkers. Say the word "horse" to anyone and they do not generally start to think of the various conveyances versus farm labor theories of equine value. They visualize a horse. Ephesians 6:12 reminds us of what we know, that satanic forces of darkness oppose us daily. We need spiritual armor to defeat such spiritual powers. To "see" that armor is a boost to faith. As you "pray" this "dress for war" pattern, visualize each piece. "Seeing" a helmet on your own head is faith inspiring when one of Satan's arrows is aimed at your head.

✎9. Read Ephesians 6:13-17 again. List each of the seven pieces of armor and briefly describe what kind of prayer emphasis might be given to each piece.

_____

_____

_____

_____

_____

_____

_____

Piece by Piece

Two men on a camping trip discussed at great length the way they put on their socks and boots. One maintained the proper way was one sock, one boot, then the other sock and at last the second boot. This he claimed meant that in an emergency he at least had one boot on. The other man urged putting on both socks then both boots. This, he explained, was symmetrical and meant that in an emergency he would never be seen in the silly posture of one boot on and the other foot naked.

Is this a silly argument? Of course! But it reveals that we are creatures of habit. Patterns of everything from brushing our teeth to getting dressed lend order to our lives. Putting on the seven items of spiritual armor in the same order every day gives structure to our need for spiritual protection. Patterning also makes the ritual familiar, comfortable and comforting, allowing us to concentrate on the value of the armor and not worrying if we left anything out.

THE SHEEP'S PRAYER

Even praise finds structure helpful. There are areas of life for which we should give God praise every day. Others change daily as some serendipitous blessing or delightful answer to prayer swoops in upon the stage of our lives demanding that we praise He who sent it. An orderly, regular, even daily, pattern of praise covers both. Such is Psalm 23. Read it now and you will easily see that there are three sections of praise—1) praise for the promises, 2) praise for the presence and 3) praise for the perpetuity.

Praise for the Promises

Sheep are not the most attractive or intelligent creatures in the world, and seeing ourselves as sheep is not all that fun. But when we do, we realize our need for a shepherd. The covenant reflection between sheep and shepherd implies a reciprocal promise. Sheep promise to follow; the shepherd, to provide, protect, and lead. When "praying" Psalm 23, begin with praise for the promises of God. A bank in Florida once advertised, "We promise performance." That is the best the world offers. God says, "I perform promises."

✎10. Identify as many separate promises as you can in Psalm 23:1-4. How many are in the first three verses?

_____

_____

_____

Praise for the Presence

As you "pray the promises" of Psalm 23:1-4 let the Holy Spirit bring the promises to mind that are specifically related to your current circumstances. The greatest promise of all is His presence. In the more difficult or painful moments of life, it is difficult to find areas to praise God for. But it is in those same moments that we can realize that the greatest blessing of all is that in such moments He is there... "Thou art with me."

✎11. Read verses 4 and 5 of Psalm 23 again. There are four promises that arise from His presence. Comfort, nurture, an anointing, and fullness are possible only because He is present. In other words, in what He does, we can see who He is. Now write a sentence about the nature of God that embraces and expresses all four.

_____

_____

Praise for Perpetuity

The final verse of the psalm brings a "foreverness" to our prayers. As you conclude each day's prayer pattern using Psalm 23, end with praise for the eternal—God's eternal goodness, His eternal mercy, His eternal blessing, and your own eternal home.

✎12. In what way does "praying the prayer of perpetuity" bring this moment into correct perspective?

_____

_____

SUMMARY

Taking into account the temptation to fall into a form of prayer while denying its power, there are great blessings in using patterns of prayer to lend form, structure, and regularity to our daily prayers. These patterns can help us "see" aspects of both petition and praise in a more understandable way, while also helping us "stay on track" by providing the very tracks themselves for the locomotive of our prayers to run on.

LET'S REVIEW

✏️1. What are some negative prayer patterns?

_____

_____

_____

✏️2. What can prayer patterns do for our prayers?

_____

_____

_____

✏️3. What areas of prayer are most enhanced by patterns?

_____

_____

_____

✏️4. Explain why one of the "patterns" of prayer described in this chapter might be most useful for:

Comfort in hardship _____

_____

_____

Strength in temptation _____

_____

_____

Power to forgive _____

_____

_____

PhotoDisc

THE PRAYER OF PRAISE: UNLEASHING THE POWER

Everyone likes to hear a sincere compliment or a genuine word of gratitude. Phrases such as "Thank you, Daddy!" "What a wonderful meal, dear. You work so hard"; "You're handsome and a great provider. What a blessed wife I am," enrich and strengthen human relationships.

Gratitude seldom comes naturally. It must be taught, required, and modeled before our children or they will be allowed to become ungrateful. Worse still, these children may grow up to become unappreciative, offensive adults, whose spouses long for appreciation and whose children become insecure, aching for approval.

Even so, we are more adept at making our desires known than praising God's majestic glory. Yet praise in our relationship with Him, as among humans, is enriching and strengthening. This vital element of prayer is ignored and undeveloped at the risk of making us into demanding children, unappreciative, and ungrateful for even God's greatest gifts.

DEALING WITH OBSTACLES TO PRAISE

Frequently, the obstacles to exuberant praise are related to who we are, and what we are experiencing, rather than to what we say we believe about the power of praise. There is hardly any area of the total prayer picture where the gap between theology and practice is any wider than at the point where praise conflicts with self and situation. Pride, circumstances, and bitterness are in opposition to unleashing the power of praise.

1. **Read John 4:1-9. Considering the ongoing tension between Jews and Samaritans, can you hear the Samaritan woman's prideful words? Identify where her racial pride shows up and paraphrase that verse in modern language.**

_____

_____

_____

_____

If Jesus had reacted to her hurt pride in John 4:9 by withdrawing or withholding the revelation He was prepared to share with her, this moment of blessing to her would have become a curse. We likewise can become so proud that we do not praise God. There can come a moment in which our prideful refusal to praise God can cause Him to resist our petitions (James 4:6).

2. **Read Matthew 6:9 and 6:13b. Rewrite those verses in the most prideful wording you can come up with.**

_____

_____

_____

_____

3. **Now, taking your rewrites in items 1 & 2 together, think of one or more modern philosophies of "vain deceit" which embody this combined attitude.**

A. _____

_____

B. _____

_____

C. _____

_____

Sometimes our circumstances loom so large that praise seems unrealistic at best, and sometimes absolutely impossible. "Doesn't God see what's happening to me?" we demand. "How can He expect me to praise Him in this?"

First of all, we must remember that God does see our circumstances, but He sees from a different perspective. Secondly, our praise must not be determined by the circumstances, but our circumstances enlightened by our praise. Here is the most important question: Which is greater, our circumstance or our praise?

4. In John 4:1-9, what particular circumstance in this Samaritan woman's life might have made it difficult for her to praise God? What could be a contemporary equivalent of her life circumstance?

_____

_____

_____

_____

Bitterness is the poisonous alloy of pride and circumstance. "How can this terrible thing be happening to ME?" Bitterness against life, God, and others will paralyze our praise. Praise can heal us by lifting us above the circumstance and the hurt, but in the initial phase there is an effort of spirit, a determination of the will that must set the process in motion. King David said, "I will bless the Lord at all times." In other words, "I am willing myself to praise the Lord all the time." Likewise, when bitterness is at the door of our hearts we must will ourselves into praise.

5. List all the parties against whom this Samaritan woman might have held bitterness. Does Jesus appear to sympathize with her with respect to any of them? From your own experience, does God sympathize with your bitterness?

_____

_____

_____

_____

PRACTICAL PRAISE: HOW TO DO IT

One minister reported visiting an elderly woman who suffered horribly from arthritis. He found her on her back porch, snapping beans, in obvious pain, her fingers hardly able to perform the task. Instead of complaining, however, she was singing "Count Your Blessings."

Sometimes those who have the most seem least full of praise and vice versa. Why? Perhaps, in part, it is learned behavior. Could it be that the over-indulged and affluent think they "have it coming," but the needy are delighted with "daily bread"?

In other words, gratitude is a learned behavior. Our spirits as well as our minds must be taught to praise.

The apostle Paul wrote in Ephesians 5:20 of "giving thanks always for all things unto God." Always? All things? That is a high bar to get over in reaching for vital praise. Paul is certainly not talking about being superficial and gleeful when a loved one dies. He speaks instead of a trained mind and spirit, disciplined to remain worshipful even in the harshest storm.

6. List three things in your own life for which you have never really thanked God. Each day for the next 7 days, praise God for each of them, observing if there are any changes in your attitude.

A. _____

B. _____

C. _____

7. List an example from Paul's life record in Acts, in which he demonstrated such a disciplined spirit. Now, record an incident from your own life in which praise seemed difficult or even impossible. How can you prepare your spirit for the next such situation?

A. Paul's experience _____

_____

B. Your experience _____

_____

C. Plan for disciplined preparation _____

_____

Sometimes we want to praise God but our "worship vocabulary" is limited. Scripture (Psalms, certainly, but not exclusively) is replete with a rich language of praise. Only if you pour into your mind such beautiful expressions of worship can the Holy Spirit summon them to your conscious mind when the storms of life are howling.

8. Would God be upset if we "learn our lines" for praise instead of coming up with our own? Why or why not? Can you give an example from the New Testament of someone praising God using the language of the Old Testament?

_____

_____

Example: _____

_____

_____

There are two levels of praise though the words may be used interchangeably without embarrassment. Praise is generally understood to be thankfulness for what God does, while worship could be defined as delighting in who God is. In other words, we praise God for blessing us and worship Him because of His attributes. To remain alive in God in the ups and downs of life you will need both. Take this little pop quiz.

✎9. Praise and Worship Quiz. Write P (praise) or W (worship) or B (both) beside each entry below.

A. The chorus—"God Is So Good"

B. Thanks for your family

C. The Doxology

D. Prayer at a funeral

E. The Song of Miriam (The Horse and Rider)

F. The hymn "How Great Thou Art"

Some have stated that to praise God differently in public than in private is sheer hypocrisy, but that is too simplistic. There are some very valid reasons why public praise may be different. For example, a man may praise his wife in public quite differently than he does in private. There is a major difference between decorum and hypocrisy. There are other reasons as well. Let's look at some of those.

A. A Different Purpose

The purpose of private praise is to build personal intimacy with God. Public praise draws the community of faith together with each other as well as with God. Mutual encouragement, energized joy for strength, and the creation of an atmosphere conducive to hearing from God corporately all happen in public.

✎10. Find a psalm that seems better suited for praise in personal devotions. Now, find one that seems perfect for a public worship service.

A private psalm: _____

_____

_____

A public psalm: _____

_____

_____

B. Right and Wrong Motives

In both public and private, one of the worst conceivable motives for praise is to impress—in public, to impress the public, and in private, to impress God! Private praise is not to manipulate God. Neither is it to "pay Him off" for delivering the goods. Public praise is not to show off. Nor is it to "rev up" a congregation. Emotional manipulations are not the same as mutual encouragement and shared joy, which are right motives for praise.

✎11. Read John 4:20,21. The Samaritan woman is asking about the correct "how" of public worship. Jesus' answer goes to motive (verse 24). To see the answer better, fill in the blank with the opposite of Jesus' words.

"God is a Spirit and they that worship Him must [not] worship Him

in _____

and in _____." John 4:24 (reversed)

Praise and Singing

Just as all squares are rectangles, but not all rectangles are squares, all singing truly offered to God is a sacrifice of praise, but not all praise is singing. Many of today's Spirit-filled churches think of all praise as being singing. Singing is a wonderful expression of praise, but just because a singer is talented does not mean the song is more wonderful to God. There are all kinds of ways to express praise to God, so some praise in public won't be linked to singing.

✎12. Name an element of your Sunday morning service in which public praise is offered apart from singing.

_____

_____

_____

_____

_____

SUMMARY

By leaping the boundaries of pride, circumstance, and bitterness, praise carries us (privately), and others with us (publicly), into God's presence as no other element of prayer can do. We must discipline our emotions and school our spirits to spend time in praising Him. If He alone is worthy of our highest praise—and He is—then to withhold it is our greatest neglect.

LET'S REVIEW

1. Name three barriers to praise.

A._____

_____

B._____

_____

C._____

_____

2. Is gratitude a natural or learned response to blessing? Explain.

_____

_____

_____

3. What is the difference between praise and worship?

_____

_____

_____

4. Where could we find appropriate language for praising God?

_____

_____

5. What is one of the worst possible motives for public praise?

_____

_____

_____

PhotoDisc

KINGDOM PRAYER: PRAYING GOD'S AGENDA

Imagine a telephone conversation with the earpiece on both phones broken. Both people might be speaking but no communication could occur. Communication is impossible without both a transmitter and a receiver. Just because a radio transmitter is broadcasting does not necessarily mean communication is happening. Until someone somewhere turns on a radio and tunes into the broadcast, the indispensable cycle of communication is incomplete.

In the same manner, prayer is incomplete until transmission finds reception—both ways. In Shakespeare's play "Hamlet" the new king of Denmark said, "My words fly up to heaven, but my thoughts stay here below." Many of us have felt this way from time to time, but how futile indeed our prayers would be if our words flew up to heaven and God's ear was turned away.

The most neglected element of prayer communication is the human receiver. If God still speaks—and we believe He does—then we must learn to listen. If our words fall on deaf ears our petitions go unmet. Worse still, if God's words fall on deaf ears, His will goes undone.

THE 100 PERCENT RULE

Here is the 100 percent rule: If we only pray God's will, He always hears us and we always have what we pray—100 percent of the time.

✎ **1. Read 1 John 5:14,15. Now fill in the blanks in your own words.**

According to 1 John 5:14,15, the _____ challenge I face in

_____ is to discover _____. Once I find that and

_____ it, I _____ God's will _____ percent of the time.

Prayer involves much more than asking God to meet our needs. It is learning to conform our desires and will to God's will. How can that happen if we cannot discern His will? Certainly the written Word of God, the Bible, is indispensable. The Holy Spirit will never lead us to any way contrary to Scripture. Only by learning to listen to the Holy Spirit will we be able to apply the Scriptures, and be guided into God's wisdom at the many crossroads we face.

Everyone wants his or her prayers answered. In fact, if the truth were known, most of us want all our prayers answered exactly as we pray them, precisely when we pray. If that were to actually happen, however, think of the mess our lives would be in. We count on God sorting through our prayers, knowing more than we do, and giving answers bigger and wiser than our questions. We depend on His being above and outside of us and our desires, not entirely subservient to us but we to Him. The sovereignty of God is not the obstacle to having our way, but the great, comforting safety net when we climb up high to make wishes known.

When God's will is apparently contrary to our own self-interests, the initial challenge is to get over to His point of view. God's sovereignty demands more than blind obedience. He wants us to accept His will as ours and pray it back to Him!

✎ **2. Read Acts 13:1-5. What do these verses indicate that enabled the church at Antioch to hear God's will for Barnabas and Saul? Explain.**

_____

_____

_____

_____

✎ **3. Read Acts 13:2,3 again. Identify the spiritual activity of the church at Antioch that enabled the believers to hear from the Holy Spirit.**

_____

_____

_____

✍4. What might the phrase, "ministered to the Lord" (Acts 13:2, KJV), mean?

_____

_____

_____

_____

Please note that after the church at Antioch had discerned God's will, they prayed and fasted more. Why might they have repeated their prayer fast then?

There are three possible answers God may give when we pray: "Yes," "No," and "Not now." The church at Antioch heard from God in community, not as "lone rangers." Perhaps God was finally answering their long-standing petition for permission to go to Seleucia and Cyprus. A "not now" became a "yes."

✍5. List an example of each divine answer that you have experienced.

Yes _____

No _____

Not now _____

REMAINING FLEXIBLE

Remembering your own carnality, be slow to "set in concrete" your current understanding of God's will. Remain flexible. God's will for your immediate circumstance changes in the light of His divine purpose. At some point God must have willed Barnabas and Saul to be at Antioch. His marching orders were to then move on to Cyprus.

✍6. Give an example of a "calling" of God that changed or developed from an "Antioch" in your life and later became a "Cyprus."

_____

_____

_____

_____

One of the reasons God sometimes answers "not now" is to let the situation change ahead of us. Another is to let us change or mature for the situation. During that time, God's answer may be, "Not now."

✎7. What circumstances or forces within us make us rigid or resistant rather than responsive and flexible to God?

_____

_____

_____

Another reason God sometimes waits to answer prayer is that at different phases of life we tend to pray differently. As we mature, so do our prayers. Elderly saints do not pray like those who are newly converted. More than simply different subjects, their prayers have different levels of faith, patience, trust, and balance.

✎8. In Acts 13 we see Saul, among others, receiving God's initial guidance for missions. Find an example later in Acts in which Paul prays differently.

_____

_____

_____

GETTING THE BIGGEST PICTURE

Imagine the opening scene of a movie. The camera is close up on two men. They are screaming at the top of their lungs. Eyes bulging, fists shaking in rage, their gaze is fixed in fury on some unseen mutual foe. You decide the movie is about these two men and some terrible adversary until the camera pulls back further and further and the two men's faces are lost in a sea of spectators. Finally, you can see the the the whole scene, the soccer game and the stadium, and you realize the two men were only extras. It's a sports movie.

As we mature in Christ and our perspective changes, our prayers change. That which we thought was so crucial turns out to be superfluous. You realize, this may not be about what you thought. Narrow vision gets in God's way and in the way of our prayers.

✎9. In order to see how perspective changes, answer the following questions about Acts 13:1,2.

How many men are mentioned? _____

Who is mentioned last? _____

At this point, has Saul had any ministry experience? _____

When the mission journey began, which man was mentioned first? _____

Who is most of the rest of the Book of Acts about? _____

Although we can center in on details, knowing the big picture gives a different perspective about the details. But vision or perspective is not the only problem. Our experiences are limited and wounded, we were looking through a clouded window, and the window is our own past. Out of our limited human experience and wounded memories, we may think we understand what God is doing when we don't.

The leaders at Antioch were not beginners. They were veterans—well-respected prophets and teachers who had discerned the will of God in the past. But did they fully realize what God was beginning among the Gentiles, or even in Paul's life? Almost certainly not. What if they measured what God was doing against their own limited experiences?

✎ **10. Think of a moment in your own life when your limited human experience caused you to miss God's greater purpose, one that you can now see. Explain how your perspective of this event has changed. How can this affect the way you pray?**

_____

_____

_____

As we pray our way past our own agendas and limited perspective, and into God's will, we must be cautious of prevailing cultural perceptions. The culture we live in may influence our prayerful submission to the sovereignty of God more than we think. What if the leaders at Antioch had yielded to the view that Gentiles had no part in their Messiah?

✎ **11. Think of an element of today's culture that could creep into the church and corrupt the way we pray.**

_____

_____

_____

✎ **12. Now think of a time when God answered your prayer exactly as you prayed. Describe the conditions of your prayer and why you feel God answered it.**

_____

_____

_____

SUMMARY

If we pray God's will, in God's timing, our prayers will be answered—100 percent of the time. The problem is not convincing God to do our will, it's praying our way into His. The barriers and hindrances to finding God's will can cause us to be bad listeners. God still speaks, but only to those who listen.

LET'S REVIEW

1. How do we put the 100 Percent Rule to work in our lives?

_____

_____

_____

_____

2. What are three ways God answers petitions?

_____

_____

_____

_____

3. Why is it important to listen to God in community?

_____

_____

_____

_____

4. Why might God delay an answer to prayer?

_____

_____

_____

_____

5. When God changes direction in our lives, why is it so hard to bear?

_____

_____

_____

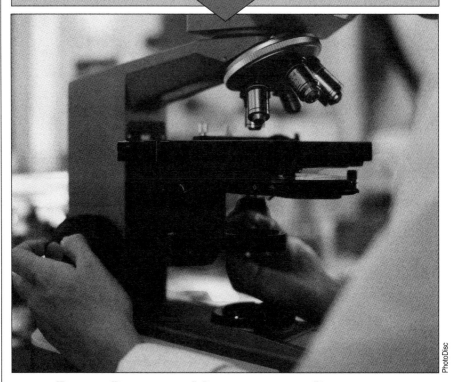

PhotoDisc

R & D FOR KINGDOM PRAYER

God, whose creative faculties cannot begin to be comprehended, who fashioned both the intricacies and the magnitude of creation, is He who hears and answers our prayers. He who first thought, then spoke light, particulate matter, and all vegetation and life into existence can answer each prayer out of that same infinite creative power.

Where we see just a brick, God sees the molecular structure of the clay, the earth from which it comes, the house it will build and the mason who will mortar and set it. God sees every family that will live in that house, their eternal destinies, and all the lives they will ever touch for good or evil. He sees the ultimate end from the tiniest beginning.

When we reach to God in prayer with an immediate need, we must remember that He reaches back to us with insight, power, and creativity beyond our wildest imaginings. God can design answers infinitely more complex and yet magnificently simpler than would ever be apparent to even the greatest human mind. He resides not only in all truth and knowledge, but also in all wisdom and creativity.

CREATIVE PRAYING

Perhaps one of the more frequently quoted verses of Scripture in the New Testament is also one of the most misunderstood. Ephesians 3:20 is often interpreted to mean that no matter how much I pray for, God will give me more. In other words, if I pray for one million dollars, God will give me three million; therefore, I should keep my requests high. But that is a very superficial view of the great Ephesians 3:20 promise. Think of Ephesians 3:20 as setting God's creativity loose in my circumstance to do not only more, but different, wider, wilder, greater, or even more unimaginable things than I prayed for.

✎ 1. Read Acts 12:1-12. Is there any record of exactly how the church prayed

for Peter? _____

Do we know, for instance, if they prayed for him to be strengthened in imprisonment,

released, or used in prison for a witness? _____

Do we know if they prayed for an angel to set him free? _____

As in all prayer, intercessory prayer and/or crisis petition we must learn to pray according to God's will, not limiting God's creativity. By trying to tell God what He should do in a situation—in essence, over-directing God—we may border on presumption, and this would limit our ability to pray in faith according to His will, limiting our usefulness in prayer. Sometimes a specific prayer agenda is called for, but on other occasions we must learn to "think differently." Instead of asking for a desired outcome, what if we were to plead for His desired outcome, leaving the results up to God?

✎ 2. Suppose you are asked to pray for a sick person. How can you pray in faith believing, without limiting God to following what you think should happen? Formulate your idea of what such an "open-ended" petition of faith might sound like.

_____

_____

_____

_____

There are two general ways in which we can know how we should pray. The first is knowing and praying God's Word, the Bible. The second is a personal word from God that He speaks to our hearts about the situations we are praying for (see Romans 8:26,27). There are moments in life when it is clear from the Scriptures that we should pray God's Word. In those instances, we need to "pray the Bible."

✎3. Read Acts 12:1-12 again. Perhaps the particulars of the church's prayers in verse 5 are not recorded because they were not specific, but general prayers based on God's Word. If a contemporary saint were in prison for the faith (as many are around the world), list some different ways you might pray, and Scriptures for each.

Prayer   Scripture

_____

_____

_____

_____

_____

_____

When God speaks to you—that is, the Holy Spirit makes a specific application of biblical truth to a situation—He will never contradict Scripture. Nor is that word from the Lord to be applied to other situations without clear direction from Him. James was killed in prison (Acts 12:2), while Peter was delivered (verses 3-11). Could James' death have been the Lord's will? Apparently, it was. Jesus himself was slain according to the predetermined will of the Father. But on some occasions, prior to His crucifixion, Jesus was miraculously delivered. He walked on water, but not on every body of water He encountered. To take a word God spoke (whether to you, someone else, or someone in the Bible) that dealt with a specific situation and then pray as though it applied to every situation is dangerous indeed.

✎4. Here are three biblical examples. Label each B for a promise from the Bible or S for a specific word God spoke about a specific situation. Explain why you labeled each as you did.

Acts 16:31 _____

_____

_____

Acts 5:15 _____

_____

_____

Acts 27:21-31 _____

_____

_____

✎5. Tell of an experience when the Lord applied a biblical truth in a specific way to a specific situation of your own.

_____

_____

_____

_____

NOW FOR R & D

Most major manufacturing and technology companies have a research and development (R & D) department. It is that department's duty to keep analyzing current methods and outcomes as well as designing new and better ones. Many people ignore R & D in prayer. As a result, they fail to keep analyzing how they pray and miss opportunities to improve outcomes. Now identify something that you have been praying about with some regularity over an extended period of time.

Let's Analyze

A certain Christian lad, a fine boy with bone cancer, was prayed for by many to the mockery of his unsaved uncle. The boy died, but at his funeral the uncle was saved and became a solid and rapidly maturing disciple. God may sometimes be about something wider and more profound than what we pray about. Could the uncle have been saved in the light of a miracle instead? Perhaps, but we only know what actually did happen. Was the soul of the uncle worth the life of his nephew? The temporal body of the boy died so that the eternal soul of his uncle might live. Does this have a familiar ring?

✎6. Research item 1: What potential scenario can you imagine if your prayers were answered, "Yes," exactly as you prayed them?

_____

_____

_____

_____

One restaurant in America made quite a success of advertising "the rudest waiters and the worst service in town." People flocked in for the novelty of having waiters insult them; of hearing a condescending maitre'd demand, "What are you doing here?"; and of cooks coming out of the kitchen to berate them for their "stupid order." Someone very creative thought of an "upside down" restaurant that really worked. Now, let your creative juices flow out into your prayer life. Is there another way to pray?

✎ 7. Research item 2: Is there another way to pray other than your customary method? Formulate a one or two sentence prayer along these lines.

_____

_____

_____

_____

Who would have dreamed that customers might like being insulted and treated rudely? Who would have imagined that an unbelieving uncle could be saved by his nephew's death? Perhaps only God. When we free our minds and spirits, God may lead us into prayer and outcomes we could never have imagined.

✎ 8. Research item 3: What might be some possible outcomes for you, others and the Kingdom if God were to "get loose" in your new prayer of Research item 2?

_____

_____

_____

_____

DEVELOPMENT: A NEW PRAYER

The development phase of R & D is the actual design and construction part. Scientists might say, "Okay, this is what we have learned in our research. Now let's build a model, try it out, test the results, and begin construction, production, and distribution." There may still be refinements, but development in general is the fleshing out of the answers gained in research.

✎ 9. Development 1: Go back and look at your "new" prayer in item 7.

Now set a development schedule for 1 week.

How many times each day will you pray it?_____

How frequently will you rewrite the prayer as it evolves in your mind and spirit?

○ Daily   ○ Once a week   ○ Twice a week   ○ More than twice a week

Sometimes the R & D department of a company discovers that once a project is near completion, another project suddenly needs to be rethought. Enclosed thinking, once reversed, can have a domino effect on our thinking. Any creative, ingenious development in one area frees energetic minds to think in a different way.

✎10. Development 2: Are there other prayer projects that you want to rethink? Name another long-prayed prayer. Now rewrite it.

_____

_____

_____

_____

A famous police detective once said that he reads back through "dead" cases every once in a while just to see if one of them comes "alive" for him. R & D departments likewise occasionally resurrect "dead" projects that with fresh thought or technological advances, suddenly seem possible again.

✎11. Development 3: Name a prayer that you used to pray with some regularity but it is no longer part of your prayer life.

_____

_____

_____

_____

Finally, when successful companies talk of R & D, they invariably speak of departments not individuals. Any sizable scientific firm that spoke of their "R & D man" would be laughed at. R & D is a corporate issue—folks working, thinking, and creatively visioning together—not as lone rangers.

✎12. Development 4: Can your prayers join with the prayers of others for increased effectiveness and multiplied creativity? How? Name one person with whom you could discuss "new" prayers.

_____

_____

_____

_____

SUMMARY

Considering the infinite creativity of the mind of God, we must seek to let the Holy Spirit enlarge our faith to pray in new ways about lingering concerns. One man prayed for many years for his son to be saved. Finally, God directed him to get seven friends to join him in praying for his daughter-in-law to be saved. In 2 weeks came the first breakthrough in years, and this, in turn, led to the salvation of the son. Research and development can take us into fresh and exciting new ways to pray.

LET'S REVIEW

1. Is there more than one way to pray about anything? Explain.

_____

_____

_____

2. How can you use God's Word to pray about a situation?

_____

_____

3. What could creative thinking do for prayer?

_____

_____

_____

4. Describe how R & D could be used to revitalize your prayers.

_____

_____

5. Why get others involved in your prayer R & D?

_____

_____

GETTING RESULTS:
PRAYING THE PRAYER OF FAITH

An American evangelist and an African pastor observed a small girl with a great burden. On her back was her baby brother, in each hand a pail of water, and on her head a tub of wet laundry, yet she walked with confident grace and apparent ease.

"She must be very strong," the American speculated. "I doubt American girls her age could manage all that." "Certainly she is strong," the African agreed. "Perhaps she is even stronger than American girls her age. But that is not her secret. She knows what American girls do not— that balance is greater than strength."

It is true. Americans tend to carry burdens out in front, in their arms, thus straining their backs. Most people in Third World countries know to get the weight directly over their center of gravity. In that way, more of the bearer's strength is under the burden, so balance becomes more important than arm and back muscles. Get the burden centered over your greatest strength—God—then keep your balance. This is a great theological truth.

THE GREATEST STRENGTH

When we start to press into God's presence with our petitions in hand, the burden may be massive. In the crises of life both strength and balance are the hardest to find. The problem usually involves how to pray in faith without questioning God's sovereignty. In Hebrews 4:16, we are told to "come boldly unto the throne of grace." Yet a wholesome fear of presumption bids us to remain reluctant to even appear to be ordering God about. The problem must be balanced over our greatest strength, which is the goodness of God. Resting in God's goodness, our burdens can be prayed through with boldness and trust in balance.

✎1. If you were asked to choose one verse in the entire New Testament that speaks only to the nature of God, what verse would you choose?

_____

What word or words in that verse describe God's character?

_____

_____

_____

✎2. How does the word(s) in that verse (item 1) encourage you to "come boldly" into God's presence?

_____

_____

Now list the opposite of that word(s) _____

What effect would that view of God's character have on holy boldness in prayer?

_____

_____

Learning to rest our burdens upon the character of God is crucial. Unfortunately some people have missed the point of Jesus' parable in Luke 18:1-8. They compare the judge in the story to God and have drawn unfortunate conclusions about His nature. But there are clear statements that reveal the true point of this parable.

✎3. Read Luke 18:1. Paraphrase in your own words how Luke explains the point of the parable before he recounts it.

_____

_____

_____

Now, as we build our platform for a strong, balanced prayer, we must "put it all together." Read Hebrews 10:19-22. Two-thirds of that platform is clear in this passage: the blood and the high priesthood of Jesus. The other third, His name, is certainly hinted at. Now read John 16:23,24. There it is! The three-ply strength upon which all boldness in prayer rests: the name, the blood, and the priesthood of Jesus Christ. By these three things we may enter in boldly before a good and loving God. Hallelujah!

✎4. The purpose of the parable of the unjust judge in Luke 18 is not to reveal the character of God, but to reveal the character of persevering prayer. Remember study 6. If God is good (and He is), and we pray in the name of Jesus, by His blood, and through His priesthood, why would Jesus teach us perseverance? Why aren't such "prayers of faith" answered immediately?

_____

_____

_____

✎5. Some have taught that once we have prayed in faith we ought never to mention it to God again. What does Luke 18:1-8 teach about this?

_____

_____

_____

Standing on our solid platform of strength and balance, we fuel our prayers with high-octane energy. Look back at study 5. Once in line with the entire realm of creation our prayers are energized God-ward with one great force. That force is visible in nature, heard in heaven, and celebrated among the saints.

✎6. What is the power source of petitioning prayer?

"Come before his presence with _____...enter

into His gates with _____, and into His courts with

_____(Psalm 100:2,4)."

At this point we are ready for the payload. We have laid the foundation, confident of God's nature and Christ's priesthood. We have been energized by singing, thanking, and praising Him in worship as we enter His presence. We are ready to unburden our hearts in prayer and hear from Him. We tell Him our cares; He tells us how to pray. If we pray that, He will answer—100 percent of the time.

✎7. Before we can know the will of God we must learn to _____

_____

_____ (study 6).

Remember the account of Christ's agony in the Garden? God was not angry when a tortured soul appealed for escape. But He was truly glorified when a yielded soul surrendered! Praying confidently in God's presence is easier once we have mixed the sublime recipe for strength and balance.

8. What is the right combination of the following in prayer?

God's _____

Christ's _____

The power of_____

Praying the_____ of the Father.

PRAYER FOCUSED MIRACLES

One Bible teacher calls miracles "the focus of power." If that is true, then miracle praying is simply confident prayer focused for miraculous results. That focusing may come about in a moment or across an extended period of time. Time is not the point, but getting prayer and the will of a mighty God in focus is. Think of this kind of prayer as a magnifying glass focusing the sun's rays on dry tinder. The sun was always there. So were the fuel and the glass. The focused combination led to powerful results.

9. Miracles of past physical healings are what some Christians think of. Healing miracles are also for today. There is no biblical evidence whatsoever that healing miracles have or will disappear from the Church until the Rapture. Name some other possible types of miracles.

_____

_____

_____

_____

10. Miracles have occurred under the ministries of such well-known healing evangelists as Kathryn Kulman or Oral Roberts. Can you name advantages for miracles occurring in a local church community without a well-known healing evangelist present?

_____

_____

_____

_____

KEEPING BALANCE TO PRAYER

There are some who take a verse from the Bible and demand that God grant to them what they demand. This is known as "hyper-faith." Although there are many promises God has made, we must recognize that God's will takes precedence over our desires and demands. The key to keeping balance in prayer is acknowledging the sovereignty of God. We dare not wave God's Word under His nose and demand our answer in our way and in our time. But we are even worse off doubting God's goodness, love, and power. His heart is toward us—He desires to bless us and grant us the desires of our hearts—and His arm is not too short—His is all-powerful. Yet we must yield our desires at the point of His sovereign will, knowing that our finite view may not reflect His plan.

✎11. Read Luke 4:3,4. Outline a flow of human reasoning showing that Jesus should have bread, and not go hungry.

_____

_____

_____

_____

Now paraphrase Christ's view of facing this crisis of need.

_____

_____

_____

To embrace a "miracle or nothing" attitude in a crisis of faith is a dangerous theological tactic that limits God. Sometimes God gives a miracle. Sometimes He bestows sustaining grace. We may be delivered from the circumstance or we may be delivered in the circumstance. If we will listen, God will direct us on how to pray. Even in the moment of praying for a miracle, God will redirect us.

✎12. Read 2 Corinthians 12:7-10. Why did God refuse to remove Paul's "thorn in the flesh"?

_____

_____

_____

_____

✎ 13. No one knows for sure what Paul's thorn was. (One theory connects the passage to Galatians 6:11.) What are some *thorns in the flesh* that people today deal with?

_____

_____

_____

_____

_____

Faith arises from our hearing God rather than His hearing us. We often think if we can just get God to listen, then our miracles will come. All the while, God may want us to ease our wounded mind and emotions into the healing bath of His loving resolution. That may mean an ultimate healing in heaven rather than a temporal one. Death is not the worst that can happen to a Christian. Pray for the miracle. Believe to the last second. But trust an eternal God with the spirits of saints, knowing He will do what is best.

✎ 14. Read 1 Corinthians 15:51-58. Imagine a certain Christian with cancer. Is it theologically proper to pray for a miracle? Yes_____ No_____

Would it be proper to go to special "healing services"?

Yes_____ No_____

Would it be proper to anoint that person in a community prayer of faith?

Yes_____ No_____

If that Christian dies anyway, would it be considered a defeat?

Yes_____ No_____

Should we continue to pray for miracles? Yes_____ No_____

SUMMARY

We must correctly balance: faith and the sovereignty of God, gifted healers and the community of faith, and miracles and the eternal. By trusting in a good and all-powerful God and through prayers offered in faith in the name of Jesus, miracles are to be expected and rejoiced in. But we must remember, God is in control and His ways and reasonings are not ours (see Isaiah 55:6-12).

Let's Review

True or False. Put a T for true or an F for false in the blank next to each of the following statements. Write an explanation for each answer.

_____ 1. The ultimate basis of all true faith is the character of God.

_____

_____

_____

_____

_____ 2. God will withhold miracles unless we praise Him correctly.

_____

_____

_____

_____ 3. If a Christian dies of illness it always means their faith was insufficient.

_____

_____

_____

_____ 4. It is always God's will for us to be delivered from suffering.

_____

_____

_____

_____ 5. Only pastors and evangelists should pray for miracles.

_____

_____

_____

STUDY 9

PhotoDisc

PRACTICAL INTERCESSION: DOING THE WORK FOR OTHERS

"Shall I hide from Abraham that thing which I do?" (Genesis 18:17). With that question God sublimely seemed to confuse the issue. Certainly there was a thinly veiled invitation to Abraham to get involved. God opened the door for Abraham to pursue negotiations. His stated purpose was obviously judgment, but He invited Abraham to appeal for mercy.

The essential motivation for all true intercession is mercy, not justice. Both mercy and justice are in God's character, but intercession is a spiritual rescue mission, an act of mercy best performed by the merciful. Just as God, by announcing judgment, obviously hoped to explore how much Abraham cared for Lot and his family, so we must care before we can intercede.

GOD SEEKS PARTNERS

Among the more intriguing elements of the Genesis 18 account is the apparent willingness, even desire, of God for partnership with Abraham. God does not need our wisdom or counsel, yet He seems to not just tolerate our participation, but also to actually encourage it. By summoning us into intercession, God invites us to partner with Him in touching the lives of others.

God does not want for power or wisdom, yet He does recruit human partners. This arises from His desire for fellowship and our need for meaning. A loving God wanting His children involved in His redemptive process is similar to a small boy "helping" his dad repair a fence. There is apparently some way in which the heart of heaven is actually moved, wants to be moved by the prayers of humans. John Wesley said, "There are some things God simply will not do until someone prays."

1. Read Exodus 32:7-14. List any similarities between this account and the Genesis 18 story.

_____

_____

_____

What is different about Moses' approach to "convincing" God?

_____

_____

_____

If God's true intent is our involvement then He must be revealing both His eventual judgment and His merciful heart to us. In the Bible we can see the wrath of God building up, as it were, behind the restrained dam of His patience. Yet His desire for the lost to be saved is just as clear. In 2 Corinthians 5:11, Paul wrote, "Knowing this judgment, we persuade men." Should not this same knowledge compel us to pray?

2. Find a passage of Scripture that reveals the ultimate judgment of God on sin.

_____

_____

Now find a passage of Scripture that reveals His desire for sinners to be saved from

His wrath._____

_____

_____

The following two questions will never be fully answered, yet they are very encouraging in their implications.

First, what is there about prayer that touches the heart of God? In other words, why prayer? We could make our desires known to God in many other ways. Why doesn't God have us drop pennies down a wishing well and call out our desires? Some write their prayers on bits of paper and stuff them in the cracks of the Wailing Wall in Jerusalem. Is that what God wants? If not, why not? God wants us to realize that relationships are not strengthened with hurried notes, but with time and communication.

The second question is this. Why does God invite us to intercede, and then perhaps delay giving the answer? There may be many reasons. Sometimes what we pray for violates someone's free will. For example, will God force salvation on someone because of our intercession? No, but He can apply unimaginable pressure, so great that salvation may seem irresistible in such a case. Time allows that pressure to build. Delay also keeps us in communication. Perhaps if God answered every prayer instantly we might not spend as much time with Him.

✎ 3. A father and his little girl sit on the front porch talking. "I have a job offer in California," he says.

Why might he tell her? _____

_____

She begins to plead not to leave her surroundings.

Why would he listen?_____

_____

_____

What is happening relationally?_____

_____

_____

_____

Why might he move the family anyway?_____

_____

_____

_____

Notice the similarities between this story and the account in Genesis 18. The father invited and valued his daughter's input on the possibility of moving, though ultimately the decision rested in his hands. God involved Abraham in His plan to destroy the cities of Sodom and Gomorrah, even though the final decision was not Abraham's to make.

✎4. Read Acts 9:1-20. Between verses 19 and 20, could Saul still have said no to Christ?_____ Have you ever known anyone so hurting, alone, confused, and afraid who said no to Christ? _____

Explain _____

_____

_____

We pray and God applies the pressure, but in the final analysis people are free, moral agents. Even some on their deathbeds resist Christ to the last. Look at the man Ananias in this story. He does not appear to be praying that Saul be saved, but seems to be arguing with God against it. But God was patient, loving, and firm, knowing Ananias' very human viewpoint was limited. God may change the way we intercede even as we pray. He may then involve us in the answer.

✎5. Record a time when you were used to help answer your own prayers for others.

_____

_____

REQUIREMENTS FOR INTERCESSORS

A young man in need of a job hurried to apply for the position advertised for a communications expert. He bristled when the interviewer summarily dismissed him as "totally unsuitable." Why, he demanded to know, since he had a bachelor's degree in communications, was he unsuitable, and how could the interviewer know that without even asking any questions?

"Because," the interviewer explained, "you did not read the ad all the way through. The communication expert we need is a deaf woman, fluent in sign language, to work with deaf elementary school girls in a residential home."

Sometimes we may be tempted to apply for a job before we know the requirements. Of course, any praying believer may and should intercede, but three qualities are indispensable for sustained success in the office of intercessor.

✎6. Considering Moses and Abraham as models, what are three qualities indispensable for intercession?

_____

_____

_____

_____

Intercession is largely investment without return, or, at least, delayed and intangible return. Imagine asking an investor to put out resources without getting anything back, or at best, without having the joy of seeing someone else blessed. Such an investor would have to be very unselfish. Intercession means giving time, energy, and emotion for someone else's benefit. It is also a quiet office. If you claim the credit you may spoil it for everyone. No one may ever know how long and hard you prayed. That requires supreme unselfishness!

7. In the Genesis 18 account, what indications do you see of Abraham's unselfishness?

_____

_____

_____

In the Exodus 32 story, are there similar indications for Moses?

_____

_____

_____

_____

The first quality, faith, is certainly required. One can hardly imagine anyone making such demanding prayer investments with little confidence in their success. This lesson is about intercessory prayer—not faith—but we need to have faith in order to be involved in intercessory prayer.

8. List at least three ways to strengthen faith.

_____

_____

_____

_____

_____

Remember Christ's parable in Luke 18 about the woman and the unjust judge (study 8)? The parable's point was not to teach about God, but about a quality revealed in the woman—perseverance. Perseverance is the great sustaining virtue of every intercessor. One man prayed for his own brother's salvation for 40 years! Remember, the first prayer of intercession is not nearly so important as the last one. To keep on praying is the intercessor's burden. Quitters are not needed. The second quality, perseverance, is required to be an intercessor.

✎9. Think again about the Genesis 18 story. How do you see Abraham's perseverance revealed?

_____

_____

_____

Recount an example of someone you know who persevered in intercession.

_____

_____

_____

A CEO, in dismissing a junior executive, said, "He wanted the title but not the job." The church has often been beset by title-hunters who want to be known for what they are not. They are glory seekers, not Kingdom activists, and they seldom accomplish more than confusing the weak. Be cautious of people who use titles like prophet, apostle, or even intercessor to enhance their reputation in the church. With the third quality of unselfishness, one can be an intercessor, perhaps even a great one, without putting it on a business card.

✎10. Look over the three stories in Genesis 18, Exodus 32, and Luke 18 (use KJV). Which of the three people in the stories is actually called an intercessor?

_____

_____

Which one used that term for himself?

_____

_____

Which person seemed to be in search of a reputation as an intercessor?

_____

_____

Before launching into the work of an intercessor, join I.A.—Intercessors Anonymous. Learn to take secret delight in observing answered prayer without seeking personal credit. Avoid all attempts to gain personal glory by reporting on your successes. Remember, other members of I.A. may have been on the job long before you showed up.

11. Read Hebrews 7:25. Who is the head intercessor?

_____

_____

To whom goes all glory, honor, and praise for all answered prayer?

_____

_____

Remember, God wants warriors not "super-spiritual" weirdos. Many have observed that when intercessors are called for, the self-glorifying and the goofy show up to cloud the issue. This tends to discourage the genuine. Watch out for hypocrisy, hyper-spiritual language, and emotional manipulations. These people must be firmly handled or authentic prayer warriors will stay home to pray.

12. Read Acts 5:1-11. What were Ananias and Sapphira really after?

_____

_____

What was their true motivation for the spiritual act of giving?

_____

_____

What gift of the spirit was important for Peter to have in the face of their unauthentic spirituality? Why?

_____

_____

_____

SUMMARY

God wants fellowship with His children. He summons us into the work of intercession. He wants us to pray for one another because this keeps us involved with each other and with Him. Jesus, our chief intercessor, wants us to imitate Him, obey Him, and give Him the glory. Faith, unselfishness, and perseverance empower the ministry of intercession. God is moved by prayer, and sometimes unless we pray He will not move at all.

LET'S REVIEW

✎ 1. If God is sovereign, why does He respond to prayer?

_____

_____

_____

✎ 2. Name three qualities of an intercessor.

_____

_____

_____

_____

✎ 3. What is the essential ministry motivation of intercession?

_____

_____

_____

✎ 4. What does God sometimes delay? Why?

_____

_____

_____

_____

✎ 5. To guard the office of intercessor from being usurped by weirdos, the church needs what gift? Explain.

_____

_____

_____

STUDY 10

DigitalVision

PRAYER EVANGELISM

On July 3, 1976, Palestine Liberation Organization terrorists hijacked a French airliner en route to Israel and forced it to land in Entebbe, Uganda, where dictator Idi Amin gave the terrorists safe haven. The PLO terrorists held the 103 passengers hostage at the Entebbe airport, demanding the release of some fellow terrorists imprisoned in Israel. Then, on July 3 and 4, a daring company of Israeli commandos raided Entebbe and rescued the hostages.

Prayer evangelism, like the raid on Entebbe, is the bold rescue work of Christian "commandos"—same motivation, same prize, same daring. Stolen people held captive by satanic forces must be rescued. Evangelism is not optional for the church. We are under orders. Prayer evangelism is, perhaps, the most ignored rescue force available to the church.

In a daring night ride and guerrilla raid, Abraham rescued his kinsman Lot (Genesis 14:1-16). The rescue was not unlike the one at Entebbe and serves as a useful model for prayer evangelism.

HOSTAGES OF HELL

Before the Civil War, slaves who swam across the Ohio River into southern Illinois were on free ground. Two groups competed for their bodies: slave hunters, who prowled the free side hoping to catch escapees; and rescuers, who welcomed them with blankets, food, and freedom.

The problem was that the poor confused slaves could not tell the difference, frequently with heartrending results.

Today the hostages of hell lost in sin cannot tell who is who. Often, swimming to the wrong camp and voice, they are kept in bondage, because the right voice and light are simply not there.

✎1. List some categories of "stolen people," people held captive by satanic forces and sin.

_____

_____

_____

_____

What right do you have to pray for them? There are two rights that give you full authority. First, these people do not "belong" to Satan, but to God. They are stolen property. Second, in Christ's name you have authority. You are not claiming them for yourself, but for their Creator and rightful Master.

✎2. Read 1 Samuel 30:1-8. David, like Abraham in Genesis, is seen rescuing hostages. Even though right is on his side, he fights discouragement. The prayer-evangelist can resist discouragement four ways. Write a promise from the Bible for each.

God is with you _____

God hasn't forgotten the hostage _____

You know saving them is His will_____

If you pray His will, you know He hears _____

KEYS TO VICTORY

When Colin Powell was chairman of the Joint Chiefs of Staff during the Persian Gulf War, he stated on multiple occasions two major reasons for victory. First, there was a clear-cut goal for the conflict. The U.S. knew what it wanted and was able to state its goals. Second, the U.S. did not act alone. Military and diplomatic forces were marshaled into an overwhelming power. The "Powell" doctrine might be stated as military action that was purposeful and powerful. Similarly, victories in prayer must be like the "Powell" doctrine. They must have purpose and power.

✎3. One key to victory through prayer is to identify the agenda—be specific about the party or parties to be taken out of hell's grip. Start by naming agencies you will commit yourself to intercede for.

A. Police

B. _____

C. _____

D. _____

E. _____

Now add individual names to your prayer attack agenda. Some creative titles for such a list can be used for keeping your prayer focused on these names, for example, "Ten Most Wanted List." Another could be the "Prayer Hit List."

✎4. Make out your own Ten Most Wanted List of people you want to see saved. These may be famous, near-famous, or known only to you.

1._____   6._____

2._____   7._____

3._____   8._____

4._____   9._____

5._____   10._____

Now, marshal your forces. Whom can you get to ride (pray) with you? You need like-minded cavalrymen (prayer warriors) who will knit their hearts and prayers with yours. These groups band together, attack hard, then go their separate ways until called into action again. You may think of using prayer groups instead of individuals. Multiple groups may even increase the overwhelming prayer force.

Smart Bombs

In Desert Storm we saw with our own eyes the deadly effectiveness of so-called "smart bombs." These efficient weapons were directed with pinpoint accuracy—even through the doorway of a factory! They were long-range, accurate, and powerful. But in order to work they required excellent intelligence gathering. A few years later, bad intelligence gathering caused the U.S. to mistakenly bomb the Chinese Embassy in Belgrade, Yugoslavia, instead of the intended target.

Many prayer groups have the opportunity to participate in intelligence gathering and prayer "smart bombs." One way would be to pray for missionaries around the world. Missionaries face numerous needs, obstacles, and the enemy while sharing the gospel. With good intelligence gathering, prayer groups can obtain information about the missionary's needs, and intercede on his or her behalf, calling in "smart bombs" from heaven against the enemy.

✎5. Select a missionary who lives far away from you.

Set up an intelligence gathering plan. What are three ways to gather up-to-date information about that missionary's needs?

✎6. How can you gather information about the country, political problems, or culture that a missionary faces?

✎7. How can that intelligence help make your prayers into "smart bombs"?

War Correspondents

From Xenophone, who rode with Alexander the Great and recorded his victories, to Ernie Pyle, who documented events of World War II, even to CNN with Desert Storm, war correspondents have been there to report it all. The agonizing nightmare of trench warfare in World War I had to be explained and made real to English shopkeepers.

Vietnam was the first televised war in history. That single fact may have determined its outcome more than the generals.

✎8. You can be your own war correspondent through a prayer diary. Recording victories and setbacks candidly for your eyes only can have many important benefits. Name some.

For your prayer group a war correspondent can serve much the same purpose. You and your team need to know of victories as they come. Have a brief praise session together occasionally and report on your Ten Most Wanted List. If necessary, get statistics from such groups as the police or school administration to help keep track of progress in areas you are praying about where these respective groups would be involved.

✐9. Remember the evangelistic outreach. How might a "prayer war correspondent" report to the group, the church, or perhaps other churches?

_____

_____

_____

CREATIVE STRATEGIES

Commando prayer units cannot afford to become predictable. They travel light, ride hard, attack without warning, and use unconventional methods. A conventional military unit could never have planned and executed the raid on Entebbe. The red tape, logistics, and traditional thinking would have put insurmountable time and execution barriers in the way of success. Likewise, today's creative prayer warriors are coming up with some unusual ways of "attacking" (praying for) their chosen "targets."

Prayer walking, for example, has become a favored methodology of some "commando units." Interceding for their high school, for example, they will walk around the school praying for the faculty, students, administrators, teams, and clubs. They pray for everything from safety to revival. It's a simple strategy popular with senior adults, housewives, and women's groups. It has also proven successful. Some schools report radical drops in crime, vandalism, violence, and drug use. Other schools have seen students experience a true encounter with God.

✐10. Using the following concepts from modern warfare, outline a corresponding prayer strategy and possible targets. Be creative.

A. Saturation Bombing_____

_____

B. Front-Line Assault _____

_____

C. Sniper Fire _____

_____

D. Surprise Attack _____

_____

In every evangelistic effort the logistical support network of prayer is so important. The Israeli planes that flew the rescued hostages out of Entebbe, Uganda, did not have enough fuel to make it back to Tel Aviv, so they refueled at Nairobi, Kenya. Backstage, unseen prayer that supports crusades, revivals, and neighborhood outreaches is indispensable.

✎ 11. Think of your own local church. What organized prayer support and/or prayer evangelism happens in any given week? Name them.

_____

_____

_____

_____

What new methods can you think of?

_____

_____

_____

_____

Before amphibious assaults of WW II were launched against the beaches of Europe and the Pacific Islands, the shoreline was shelled intensely. This was to "soften up" resistance so that the frontline troops would not be exposed to quite so much danger. In the same fashion, prayer warriors can "soften up" resistance to an evangelistic outreach at your church, by assaulting the enemy with prayer.

✎ 12. Come up with a simple strategy for "preparing the beaches" for your youth group to land.

_____

_____

_____

Did you remember to identify the specific target? What is it? _____

_____

_____

SUMMARY

We are responsible to be involved in rescuing the hostages of hell. Despite discouragement, setbacks, and hardships, these hostages must be snatched away from satanic forces. Believers have the authority in Jesus' name and responsibility under Scripture to pray the wanderer home. One creative way to think of this is as a military campaign. Exciting ways of praying locally and abroad are waiting to be explored and practiced by innovative prayer warriors.

LET'S REVIEW

Circle one of the choices in each of the following statements. Explain your answers.

1. Prayer evangelism is mostly _defensive_ or _offensive_.

_____

_____

_____

2. _General_ or _specific_ prayer is most effective.

_____

_____

_____

3. We _can_ or _cannot_ know if it is God's will for particular lost people to be saved.

_____

_____

_____

4. Prayer evangelism is more effective when done _alone_ or in _community_.

_____

_____

_____

5. Recording victories is a _waste of time_ or _encouraging to the troops_.

_____

_____

_____

STUDY 11

PhotoDisc

THE PRAYER SUPPORT TEAM

With the battle raging in the valley below them, three men watched from the hillside. Moses, in the middle, knew that as long as he kept his arms raised the Hebrews would win. If his arms fell his army would also fall. Aaron and Hur knew it as well. They also knew their leader's weary arms could not remain aloft without help. Each man grabbed an arm and held it up. Their supportive strength, as much as Moses' anointing, was the cause of their victory (see Exodus 17:8-16).

Aaron and Hur are the perfect role models for the prayer support team and their work. The prayer support team is the wall of fire around leaders, a hidden and humble strength that keeps leaders' arms in the air and their anointing fresh. No pastor, Christian politician, evangelist, or missionary should face ministry or life without the support of the "Order of Aaron and Hur."

Families, as well as churches and ministers need "Aarons" and "Hurs." They are needed to stand in supportive prayer around children, homes, and extended families. No marriage, new job or business venture should go forward without an "Aaron" on the right and a "Hur" on the left interceding in prayer.

THE VIRTUES OF AARON AND HUR

In this brief, but powerful portrait of Aaron and Hur supporting Moses, we can clearly see the virtues needed in a prayer support team. This important team must be loving, supportive, and humble. Aaron and Hur kept Moses central. They remembered their role and stood in reverence of his position. Their strength became his strength.

✎1. Does your pastor have a prayer support team? He must have a prayer support team who do not envy his leadership. Why would it be dangerous for those who pray for him to envy him?

_____

_____

_____

_____

The prayer support team must also be people of humble faith. Aaron and Hur saw the connection between what they did and the victory below, yet they laid no claim on the credit. Moses was the anointed leader; Joshua did the fighting. "All we did," they might have said, "was give our prayerful support."

✎2. Why would the "internally motivated" rather than "reward motivated" be wise choices for this prayer support team?

_____

_____

_____

_____

Aaron and Hur must have been emotionally as well as spiritually encouraging to Moses. To see them there, to sense their strength, to feel their strong hands holding his tired arms, that must have made him feel loved and cared for. It was a spiritual moment to be sure, but must also have been a very emotionally fulfilling moment, as well.

✎3. Should a prayer support team care for their leader emotionally as well as spiritually? Explain.

_____

_____

_____

Strike the shepherd, and the sheep will flee. That very truth, known to Satan as well as believers, exposes your pastor to more danger than anyone in the church. Satan knows that if he can defeat, discourage, tempt, or destroy your pastor, he can pull many down with him. Your pastor also knows this, yet he may find it awkward to ask for support. You may want to suggest it to him.

✎ **4. List at least three stress points where your pastor or any pastor needs constant prayer support.**

_____

_____

_____

_____

_____

Each of these points require special, sensitive, specific prayer, not a general "God bless the pastor" prayer.

✎ **5. Experiment now. Pray for each need listed in item 4. Let the Holy Spirit guide you. Out loud, with love, humility, and concern, support your pastor with prayers about these needs. (This item requires no writing. Just prayer.)**

Remember these needs are just the tip of the iceberg. Your pastor has unique needs that change every day. He needs great energy and vision. His anointing for preaching and ministry must be prayed for. There will also be temptations. Pray for his safety.

Nothing can defeat any of us like family issues.

✎ **6. Write a prayer for your pastor's family.**

_____

_____

_____

_____

INTERCESSION FOR LEADERS

Now, choose two other leaders, one political and one institutional. The Bible teaches us to pray for our leaders. Sometimes we are tempted to pray the rabbi's prayer from the musical Fiddler on the Roof, "May God bless and keep the Czar...far away from us." Understandable? Yes, but leaders from the president to the county commissioner need real prayer. And God wants you to pray for them.

✎7. Prayer needs to be made for leaders in the area of salvation, wisdom, support staff they select, protection, etc. Select one leader and write a brief prayer for him or her.

_____

_____

_____

_____

Those who counsel leaders have the power of influence. We must pray for our leaders' advisors and assistants. Pray that they will be surrounded by wisdom and integrity. Pray for justice and mercy.

✎8. What does a "hedge of thorns" prayer mean to you and how could you use it for a leader (see Hosea 2:6)?

_____

_____

Institutional leaders like school principals, police chiefs, or judges need prayer. Employers seldom get the supportive, loving prayers of their employees—whether they deserve it or not. Often, as they prosper, grow in wisdom, and walk worthy of their calling, we find peace and blessing.

✎9. List the names of four institutional leaders for whom you have never prayed.

1. _____

2. _____

3. _____

4. _____

FAMILY PRAYER SUPPORT

There is no greater strength or protection for a family than prayer. Prayer should be uniquely designed out of sensitivity to constantly changing realities in the various family members' lives. Despite your prayers, evil influences may attempt to invade your family.

During the Spanish Civil War of 1936, the term *"fifth-column agent"* was coined. The term referred to undercover agents who operated within enemy ranks to undermine its cause. The agents' work included spying, sabotage, propaganda, agitation, and infiltration. As believers, some situations—including family circumstances—require a "fifth-column agent" mentality.

10. In what way can a believing prayer warrior in a family of unbelievers work as a spiritual "fifth column agent" for the kingdom of God?

_____

_____

_____

In item 8, we mentioned the "hedge of thorns" prayer. This prayer is to erect a spiritual barrier so family members will be prevented from seeking out or being a part of questionable influences. In addition, any family member who starts out of the hedge will likewise be pricked and decide not to exit its protection. Many parents pray this daily for their entire family and for each child.

Sometimes this kind of praying needs to get specific and "ruthless." Many parents pray too "nicely." When an evil influence begins to cultivate a relationship with anyone in your family, pray "ruthlessly." Pray that the people who are evil influences will argue. Pray they will be shown to be disappointing, unrewarding, or untrustworthy. Pray they will show up for a date with bad breath, or that the car will break down, or that they will fall in love with someone else. Don't pray nice!

11. Write a "ruthless" prayer for the following example. Your grown daughter is in a job where her married boss is sexually harassing her.

_____

_____

_____

_____

Now, make up a realistic situation and a prayer to fit it.

Situation: _____

_____

_____

Prayer:_____

_____

_____

_____

PRAYER SUPPORT INVENTORY

1. Who provides the major prayer support for your extended family?

_____

2. What is the most frequent prayer you yourself pray for your family?

_____

3. Is there a situation existing in your family now that calls for "ruthless" prayer?

_____

4. Is there a political leader for whom you regularly pray?

_____

5. Do you know of a political or institutional leader with a prayer support team?

_____

6. Do you pray regularly and frequently for your pastor?

_____

7. Does your pastor have a prayer support team?

_____

8. Are the mature, balanced saints of the church on this prayer support team?

_____

SUMMARY

As Aaron and Hur kept Moses' arms aloft to defeat the Amalekites, prayer support teams can strengthen and encourage leaders today. Pastors, politicians, and leaders of every kind need such teams. These teams should not draw hyper-spiritual weirdos, but mature and balanced believers. Families need prayer support even more than governments. Satan hates the family and will send his agents to destroy it. The Lord is a hedge of thorns and a wall of fire around His people. Pray that hedge into place and keep it there.

LET'S REVIEW

1. What was the connection between Aaron and Hur to Moses and to the consequence to the battle?

_____

_____

_____

2. What three virtues are most critical for the order of Aaron and Hur?

_____

_____

_____

3. Should your pastor get more prayer than anyone else in your church? Explain.

_____

_____

_____

_____

4. Why is prayer for political leaders a "smart" prayer?

_____

_____

_____

_____

5. Do some Christians pray too "nice" for their families? Explain.

_____

_____

_____

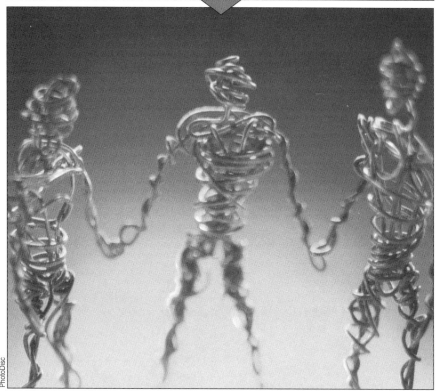

PhotoDisc

THE CREATIVE CORPORATE PRAYER CLOSET

Veterans of Pentecost, yet in deep need of a fresh touch from the Holy Ghost, these early believers gathered for prayer together. In Acts 4:24, the Scripture says, "They lifted up their voice... ." There is a wonderful moment when multiple voices become one voice, and that is the moment when God shakes the place and pours out His Spirit afresh. We all need a personal prayer life, but unified prayer with others is powerful and effective.

In this closing lesson we will consider a variety of ideas for energizing corporate prayer. You should know this, however. This lesson is not nearly so concerned with informing, as with inspiring or even provoking. The point is to provoke you, your class and/or church to find your own exciting, creative ways to get as many as possible into the corporate closet.

HELPS FOR BUILDING UNIFIED CHURCH PRAYER

Have you ever listened to a congregation drone through the Lord's Prayer, apparently without connecting to it spiritually? Discouraging, isn't it? Or perhaps you have peered into an unused prayer chapel. Signs of neglect were everywhere. It did not take great discernment to see that a formal nod was paid to prayer but it wasn't really happening there.

✎ 1. Read Acts 4:23,24. Why did they gather together? What strength was in that? What risk did they run?

_____

_____

_____

_____

One prayer idea finding a true resurgence among many churches is the "prayer room" concept. Dedicated space, equipped with such things as prayer cards, pictures of missionaries and others, lists of needs, and even praise music playing softly can help people pray. A method found useful in many prayer rooms is "stations." Each station would have a different focus for prayer. A person develops a pattern for prayers as he or she moves from station to station, praying through the concern at each.

✎ 2. What advantage can you see for using "stations" in a church prayer room?

_____

_____

_____

Name five "stations" you might propose:

1. _____

2. _____

3. _____

4. _____

5. _____

A general law of leadership is that the rank and file will seldom, if ever, move ahead of leadership. This means that if the prayer room is to become part of functional church culture, it must be used and referenced from the pulpit and other public settings by the pastoral staff and leadership.

✐3. How else could leaders help to get prayer room use into the "corporate culture" of a church?

_____

_____

_____

_____

Printed material for prayer is being used more and more by praying churches. One church distributed prayer tents that said "Pray First." They were everywhere— in the church offices, conference rooms, classrooms, and fellowship hall. They were on many dining tables of members as well. One church in Texas gave out laminated "prayer cards" with a printed prayer for a blessing on one side and the "sinner's prayer" on the other.

✐4. What are the benefits of such printed prayers?

_____

_____

Any possible negatives?

_____

_____

THE FORGOTTEN GIANT: PRAYER MEETINGS

In some churches prayer meetings have become relics of the past. In others, and what may be worse, they are dead, uninspiring, and poorly attended. Still others call certain gatherings "prayer meetings," but they are more like Bible studies or musical worship. Perhaps this unfortunate degeneration resulted from our inability or unwillingness to make a fresh effort to bring creativity and imagination to a biblical concept (Acts 4). Prayer meetings are 2,000 years old—but we must make them alive in the 21st century with new ideas and fresh approaches.

✐5. List four possible names for a prayer meeting that could be used to emphasize the purpose of the meeting.

_____

_____

_____

_____

Now, challenge yourself and any traditionalism. Is conducting a vital prayer meeting more or less important than simply calling it a prayer meeting?

_____

_____

Why might a new name help?

_____

_____

_____

One way that some churches are freshening up their prayer meetings is by using them as "called" meetings—changing the format, keeping them as unique, special gatherings rather than scheduling them in a regular time slot. There are advantages and disadvantages to this approach, but one major problem that it helps diffuse is that of scheduling for failure. A regular prayer meeting scheduled every Wednesday has no fixed ending date. When will it stop? When no one comes anymore? By calling one prayer meeting or a series there is more of a tendency to schedule for success.

6. List three times of day, days of the week, groups or settings that have not been tried in your church. Here's one idea to get you started.

A. Men's Prayer Meeting for three Saturdays at 7:00 a.m. in the gym

B. _____

C. _____

D. _____

Idea Mart #1

7. List 10 unique ideas for lifting up prayer, reminding people to pray, or in any way encouraging prayer in your church. Make at least five of them for the wider community.

1._____   6._____

2._____   7._____

3._____   8._____

4._____   9._____

5._____   10._____

Now make a budget. Beside each one above place a loose estimate of what it might cost to actually do it.

Idea Mart #2

A church in Georgia studied Joel 2:12-17 and called seven "solemn assemblies" (every Thursday for 7 weeks) in preparation for a revival. Southeastern College in Lakeland, Florida, made prayer and fasting its emphasis for an entire academic year. The students made prayer and fasting pledges, filled out fulfillment cards as they met their pledges, and graphed the results on a huge board in the chapel. One night the college scheduled an "all night prayer meeting" and served breakfast at 6:00 a.m. Seven hundred college students prayed all night! Prayer campaigns, New Year's watch night services, prayer breakfasts, and many other ideas are out there and in your imagination.

✎8. Come up with five ideas for stimulating group prayer.

_____

_____

_____

_____

_____

One reason prayer meetings lack zing is that the prayer element of many worship services is either short-changed, perfunctory, or both. Almost all Spirit-filled churches today have more music than prayer.

✎9. How many minutes are spent in serious prayer in your main worship service?

_____

In announcements? _____

In music? _____

How could more intense prayer be encouraged? Write out one specific idea.

_____

_____

_____

THREE VITAL PRAYER ELEMENTS

There are three elements of prayer vital to the life of the church: fasting, forgiveness, and meditation. Fasting brings an intensity and concentration to prayer that nothing else provides, especially when groups encourage each other through a declared fast.

One church that had experienced a very troubled season of divisiveness called three Saturday morning "prayer and forgiveness" gatherings that broke the spirit of woundedness.

✎ 10. Analyze your own experience with fasting. Be honest! Have you ever fasted even one meal? _____ (Sleeping through breakfast doesn't count!) Do you fast regularly?_____

How, when? _____

_____

What is the longest fast you have ever completed?_____

Has your church or group ever called a fast? _____

Meditation is also a lost art of prayer. Because of an unfortunate association with Eastern religions, many believers have never participated in Christian meditation. David meditated (Psalm 1; 63; 119; 143); Isaac did, (Genesis 24:63); and Paul encouraged it (1 Timothy 4:15). The idea, simply put, is to concentrate with such intensity on a verse of Scripture, or an aspect of God's truth until it comes alive in you at a new level.

✎ 11. Choose one brief verse of Scripture. Now divide the verse into seven parts. (i.e., Revelation 1:18a) "I am/ he that/ liveth/ and was dead/ and behold I am alive/ forever more/ Amen/ and have the keys of death and hell (KJV)." Meditate, think on it intensely, roll it around in your mind, dwell on each section for 1 day this week.

My verse: _____

_____

_____

_____

_____

SUMMARY

Group prayer, especially but not exclusively in times of crisis, is encouraging and empowering just as it was in Acts 4. It must, however, be intentional, multi-faceted, and organized. Special series, one-time meetings, and campaigns all add spice to corporate prayer. Fasting, forgiveness, and meditation can turn on the power in wonderful ways.

Prayer is not just for the stratospheric saints among us. It is for all believers. Be practical, down to earth, creative, and even ingenious. Pray together, pray loud, pray silently, pray and fast, pray and meditate, pray in old ways, or pray in new ways, but however you do it—don't just talk about it! PRAY!

LET'S REVIEW

Answer the following questions. Explain your answers.

1. Is prayer a high priority in your church? _____

_____

2. Does your church have a prayer room? _____

_____

3. Is it high profile and well used? _____

_____

4. Are special prayer meetings designated and called? _____

_____

_____

5. Is fasting an important part of your church's values? _____

_____

_____

6. Are "fasts" called for and led? _____

_____

_____

7. Have you heard meditation taught and/or modeled? _____

_____

_____

8. Rank the following (1-5) among the priorities of your church.

Finances _____

Music _____

Preaching/teaching _____

Prayer _____

Fellowship _____

Additional titles in the SPIRITUAL *DISCOVERY* SERIES

The Foundations Track

A New Way Of Life by Robert L. Brandt introduces new converts to the major practices and beliefs of the Pentecostal/Charismatic community. The biblical basis of salvation, water baptism, communion, the baptism in the Holy Spirit, church membership, stewardship, and evangelism are discussed. Additional studies detail ways to become an effective Christian through the discipline of Bible reading and prayer, and developing daily standards of conduct.

SG 02-0104
LG 02-0204

Baptized In The Spirit by Frank M. Boyd is an updated and reformatted version of a Pentecostal classic. Users of this title will come to understand the nature of the Holy Spirit, His ministry, the biblical basis for the baptism in the Holy Spirit, the initial evidence, how to receive, means of staying full, and the various gifts of the Spirit and their proper usage.

SG 02-0111
LG 02-0211

A Heart For The Lost by Robert L. Brandt will motivate individuals to prepare for the task of evangelizing. Brandt leads individuals into an exploration of the basis of evangelism, and then proposes a biblical standard for performing the task. Those who use *A Heart For The Lost* will discover that evangelism is not an activity to be feared, but a natural extension of one's Christian experience.

SG 02-0113
LG 02-0213

Spiritual Devotion by Dr. Nathan H. Nelson explores the art and discipline of developing one's spiritual relationship to God. This study challenges individuals to go beyond mechanical devotional routine toward intimacy with their God. Those who seek a deeper spiritual devotion will find this title refreshing, insightful, and rewarding.

SG 02-0107
LG 02-0207

Biblical Foundations by Donald F. Johns explores 13 commonly held Pentecostal beliefs and leads the learner into an understanding of the biblical basis for each. Topics include salvation, water baptism, and the baptism in the Holy Spirit.

Living By The Spirit by Lorraine Mastrorio introduces readers to the Spirit baptism experience, describes the fruit of the Spirit, and encourages them to allow God to use them through the supernatural and ministry gifts. It provides direction for Pentecostal believers in their quest to live a Spirit-led lifestyle.

SG 02-0118
LG 02-0218

Missions: Home And Abroad by Delmer Guynes is a challenge to the Church throughout the world to be missions-minded. Jesus' Great Commission is a command to every believer and to every church—all must be actively involved in missions efforts both in their homeland as well as in foreign countries. Guynes explores the means, the call, the resources, and the patterns for the missions task God has presented His Church.

SG 02-0123
LG 02-0223

SG 02-0126
LG 02-0226

Roots Of Pentecostal Belief by John W. Wyckoff is a journey through the ages to discover how today's Pentecostal beliefs have been a standard of belief in the past. By looking at five different eras of Church history—the Early Church, the Reformation, Revivalism, the Holiness Movement, and Evangelicalism—Pentecostal believers will see their spiritual heritage develop through the spiritual movements of the past. They will also understand how these beliefs form the foundation of the biblical beliefs Pentecostals hold dear today.

SG 02-0132
LG 02-0232

Additional titles in the SPIRITUAL  *DISCOVERY* SERIES

The Life Issues Track

Facing Midlife Challenges by Dr. Raymond T. Brock explores the transitions of life, personal fulfillment, physical changes, sexual adjustments, mortality, and more. This book is good for those in the midst of midlife or approaching it.

SG 02-0115
LG 02-0215

SG 02-0117
LG 02-0217

One For The Lord by Dr. Earl G. Creps helps singles examine their position in the world, their place in the Church, and their relationship to God. Learners will be encouraged to discover God's purpose and fulfillment in their lives.

SG 02-0106
LG 02-0206

Parenting: The Early Years by Kay E. Marchand is designed to address issues confronted by new parents—prenatal through preschool. Various aspects of parenting including making preparations for a newborn, introducing a child to Jesus, proper nutrition, discipline, learning stages, developmental stages, and communication patterns are explored.

SG 02-0109
LG 02-0209

Parenting The Elementary Child by Dr. Raymond T. Brock addresses developmental stages, discipline techniques, developing a spiritual climate in the home, the birthing order, financial stress, and intimacy challenges faced by parents during this ever-changing time. Additional studies focus on the unique challenges of the one-parent family, the blended family, the traditional family, and families with exceptional children.

SG 02-0130
LG 02-0230

Stepparenting by Dr. Billie Davis gives much-needed help concerning an increasingly common situation in contemporary society. Dr. Davis' insights and suggestions will help those who face this situation to plan and execute proper relations within their stepfamily. Dr. Davis provides hope for those who feel overwhelmed by encouraging them to walk step-by-step along this challenging path in the strength and power of the Holy Spirit.

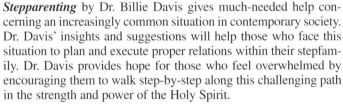

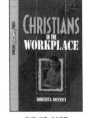

SG 02-0127
LG 02-0227

Christians In The Workplace by Roberta Bonnici exhorts the believer to worship God in the workplace through their Christian conduct and attitude toward those with whom they work. Bonnici offers practical advice which will help Christians as they encounter challenges to their faith and temptations to compromise their personal values. Those who use this book will understand the origin of work and its value.

SG 02-0129
LG 02-0229

Building Healthy Marriages by Terry Bryant challenges husbands and wives to apply biblical truths to the God-ordained relationship of marriage. Bryant offers practical insights on such topics as what it means to leave and cleave, how two people can truly achieve oneness, how to be a person of commitment, how to employ proper and effective communication, and what it means to grow spiritually as a couple

Additional titles in the SPIRITUAL Discovery SERIES

The Book Study Track

How To Study The Bible by G. Raymond Carlson introduces the learner to the background of our present Bible, rationale for studying the biblical text, and techniques to enrich the believer's Bible study experience. Users will explore the inductive method of Bible study, topical study procedures, biographical studies, word studies, and the synthetic method of Bible study.

SG 02-0108
LG 02-0208

Bible Prophecy by Dr. Stanley M. Horton involves the learner in an investigation of end-time events. They will discover the purpose of prophecy, methods of interpretation, and specific events which the Bible clearly predicts. *Bible Prophecy* demystifies prophecy and encourages learners to live with expectancy and faithfulness as they await Christ's coming.

SG 02-0105
LG 02-0205

Acts: To The Ends Of The Earth by Emil Balliet is an inductive study designed to guide the learner toward an understanding of the historical context and theological content of the Book of Acts. Those who engage in this study will be challenged to discover and apply eternal principles introduced by the Holy Spirit through the First Century Church.

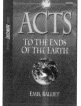

SG 02-0112
LG 02-0212

Letters To Corinth by Dr. Charles Harris engages the learner in an exegetical examination of the letters of 1 and 2 Corinthians. This series of studies provide answers to various issues faced by local churches throughout history including disunity, immorality, spiritual excess, faulty theology, suffering, and stewardship.

SG 02-0116
LG 02-0216

Letters From Prison by Lauren W. Orchard examines Paul's letters to the churches of Ephesus, Colosse, and Philippi and to Philemon. It shares God's design for a personal relationship with God and with those whom believers fellowship.

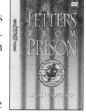

SG 02-0121
LG 02-0221

Romans by G. Raymond Carlson examines Paul's letter to the Romans introducing learners to many of the theological concepts vital to the Christian experience such as original sin, sanctification, justification, Redemption, and the Atonement.

SG 02-0119
LG 02-0219

Writings of John by Robert Berg sheds new light on the time and culture in which these vital books of the Bible were written. Dr. Robert Berg's unique approach will give you a deeper understanding of the Gospel of John as well as insight into First, Second, and Third John. The Writings Of John leads readers into the Scriptures to learn Who the Word of God is, how Jesus is just like His Father, what the Holy Spirit has been sent to accomplish, how to remain in Christ, when Jesus accomplished His earthly mission, and how to know who "true" Christians are.

SG 02-0131
LG 02-0231

Additional titles in the SPIRITUAL  SERIES

The Critical Concerns Track

SG 02-0110
LG 02-0210

Sanctity Of Life by Michael H. Clarensau focuses on the biblical perspective regarding current life issues facing today's Church. Issues examined include the value of life, the power of death, abortion, birth control, genetic engineering, suicide, murder, capital punishment, genocide, and euthanasia.

SG 02-0114
LG 02-0214

Combating The Darkness by John T. Maempa is designed to equip the believer to recognize and respond appropriately to spiritual attacks. Maempa avoids sensationalism by directing the learner to biblical passages that provide a firm foundation on which to stand strong in the midst of spiritual warfare.

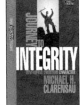

SG 02-0120
LG 02-0220

Journey To Integrity by Michael H. Clarensau proclaims the importance of character in the Christian's life. Clarensau recognizes integrity is a process and provides a plan which, if followed, will lead to the user's desired destination.

SG 02-0122
LG 02-0222

Recovery For Codependency by Steven E. Stiles is a step-by-step path to recovery from negative behaviors and addictions. It is for those personally struggling with an addictive behavior or assisting someone else in his or her struggle.

SG 02-0125
LG 02-0225

Managing Stress Through Positive Christian Living by Paul A. Lee and Mark & Carole Ryan explains that stress does not have to control our lives. By enriching our relationship with God, we can learn to change our responses and gain control over stress.

SG 02-0124
LG 02-0224

In Search Of Truth by Paul W. Smith, Clancy P. Hayes, and Kerry D. McRoberts provides an overview of the distinctions between Christianity and Judaism, Mormonism, Islam, Atheism, Spiritism, the New Age Movement, and other groups. It will help Christians respond appropriately to individuals within these groups.

SG 02-0128
LG 02-0228

Music God Likes by Dr. Joseph Nicholson examines the wide variety of musical styles employed by the Church today. He encourages his readers to expand their musical options and appreciate musical styles they may have previously avoided in both personal and corporate worship.